Tim Ewbank and Stafford Hildred

ROGER DALTREY

THE BIOGRAPHY

PORTRAIT

CONTENTS

ACKNOWLEDGEMENTS

The authors wish to express their deep gratitude to the many individuals who have made this book possible. Heartfelt thanks go to all those who have figured in Roger Daltrey's life who agreed to be interviewed for this book.

For their co-operation, help and encouragement, special thanks go to: Geoff Baker; Dave and Sue Batchelor; John Blake; Jay Bowers; Danaë Brook; Alan Brooke; Mel and Ruth Chapman; Tom and Mags Condon; Keith Cronshaw; Carrie Davies at the Halfmoon, Putney; Richard Dawes; John and Wendy Dickinson; Ingrid Dodd; Ian Dowell; Karen Dunn; Alan Durrant; Ken Eastaugh; Jane Ennis; the late John Entwhistle; Bill Eve; Carole Anne Ferris; Peter and Janet Garner; Phillip Garrahan; Rod and Joy Gilchrist; David and Sally Gritten; Don Hale; Richard Hall; Philip and Ann Hammond; Jim and Jorma Hampshire of Canterbury Rock; The History Channel; Kathryn Holcombe; Lorinda Holness; Mike Hope; Jerry Johns; Allan Jones, editor of *Uncut*; Paula Jones; Selina Julien; Pat and Nick Justice; Fergus Kelly; Barry Kernon; Alan Kingston; Simon Kinnersley; Fiona Knight; the late Kit Lambert; Ray and Janet Lewis; Moira Marr; Bryan and Vicki Marshall; Fraser Massey; Ian McLagan; Charles McCutcheon; Joanna Mitchell; the late Keith Moon; Neal Moyse; Barry Munslow; Garth and Davina Pearce; Sean and Debbie Pouley; Keith Richmond; Ken Russell; Alison Sturgeon; Freda Tallantyre; Alistair Taylor; Teenage Cancer Trust; Alison and Paul Tissington; Lynn Trunley-Smith; Francis White of The Rollin Stoned and Lesley White.

The authors would like to acknowledge as important sources:
Guitar World; Sound International; Woman's Own; VH1; Q Magazine; Rolling Stone; The Sun; News of the World; Daily Mirror; Daily Mail; Daily Express; New Musical Express; Melody Maker; Goldmine; Los Angeles Times; Now; Simon Goddard's *Uncut* interviews; *Before I Get Old - The Story of The Who* by Dave Marsh; and *The Kids Are Alright* DVD.

Special thanks to the irrepressible Alasdair Riley for his generous access to the late Kit Lambert's personal recollections.

Tim Ewbank would especially like to thank Keith Altham for his invaluable insights, and for his tickets to two concerts by The Who at their peak which will always live in the memory. Tim also wishes to thank his guitar teacher Rob Urbino for his exceptional knowledge and enthusiasm, and his encouragement to try a few of Pete Townshend's power chords.

Prologue

Look at me. I'm a funny little geezer, really. Skinny. Only five feet seven inches. Bow legs and a lopsided walk. But I was born with a star presence. That's an indefinable quality, but I've got it.

Roger Daltrey

The long queue snaking around the side of the building in London's Charing Cross Road tells its own story. The venue is the Mean Fiddler and the event is a London convention for fans of The Who. Two members of the band, Keith Moon and John Entwistle, are both dead, but the message for the assembled fans is that Roger Daltrey, Pete Townshend and The Who live on.

It's exactly 40 years since Townshend delivered his short, sharp, three-chord shock as The Who's opening salvo on disc. Four decades have passed since Roger Daltrey sang Townshend's words of teenage angst and inarticulate frustration for that first record 'I Can't Explain'.

Once inside the Mean Fiddler, it's like a flashback in time. On the walls are posters from decades ago advertising upcoming concerts by The Who, Townshend pictured with trademark arm upraised on high over his guitar. Specially erected monitors are screening vintage, possibly bootleg, footage of the band, filmed adoringly by some fan, showing Roger cockily strutting the stage swinging his microphone lead as though about to lasso a steer.

In one corner of the club bidding has started for a rare copy of *Ready Steady Who!*, an EP issued on 11 November 1966. Its cover picture shows four very young musicians, Roger looking almost angelic, piercing blue eyes gazing out under golden hair combed forward Beatles-style. Two of the tracks are 'Bucket T' and 'Barbara Ann', recorded as sops to the musical tastes of Keith Moon, The Who's long-dead, lamented, demonic drummer, a fanatical devotee of California's surf sounds of the 1960s.

At another table fans are jostling for prospective purchases of concert programmes and pictures of Pete Townshend in mid-air scissors kick, the late John Entwistle leaning deadpan up against his Marshall amp, Moon with drumsticks a blur, and Roger in his pomp, hair a mass of curls, frilled buckskin jacket open to reveal his taut, lean torso.

At the bar the talk, in hushed tones, is of sadness at the quite recent death of Entwistle, The Who's bassist. 'But doesn't Roger look good,' says one fan brightly, wearing a T-shirt with a colourful archery target design on the front, sixties Mod-style. 'I mean, look at Rog. You'd never think there was just a few months in age between him and Keith Richards of the Stones, now would you?'

That same night, some nine miles across town, just over the River Thames and close to the point where the Oxford and Cambridge crews start their annual boat race, the popular Half Moon pub-cum-music venue in Putney is packed with punters listening to a tribute band called Who's Who. Their set is as faithful a reproduction of Who numbers as they can muster over two frantic hours, and the singer has Roger Daltrey's distinctive on-stage mannerisms off to a T, even if he inevitably, yet understandably, falls a decibel and a semitone short when it comes to matching his bloodcurdling scream in the middle of his band's version of 'Won't Get Fooled Again'. The audience, many of whom are teenagers, know all the words and sing along at appropriate moments.

Across the Atlantic, for millions of Americans Roger's singing of 'Won't Get Fooled Again', with its obvious message, remains the abiding memory of the charity concert for New York that was held after the desperate events of 9/11.

That same day, in the London offices of Roger's management, plans are under way for he and Pete Townshend to team up for yet another fund-raising concert for the Teenage Cancer Trust to which Roger, cruelly scarred by living with cancer within his own family, is so deeply committed. There's also a remarkable offer to consider: an invitation to The Who to play at the 2004 Isle of Wight festival in front of 60,000 fans, 34 years after they first made a memorable appearance there.

On this very same day a 22-year-old disc jockey in Ohio is telling his listeners that there has never been a better group than The Who, and that there never will be. 'They will never f-f-f-fade away,' he says, echoing the way Roger stutteringly sang it all those years ago. To prove it, the DJ says, he's going to play two hours of non-stop Who.

In Australia, rumours are spreading among devotees of The Who that Roger and Pete are set to play some concerts 'down under', more than three decades after they left the country in disgrace after a riotous tour. 'You have behaved atrociously while you've been here and we hope you never come back,' was the telegram Australia's Prime Minister, Senator John Gorton, sent Roger and Co. after the mayhem and misbehaviour culminated in Keith Moon smashing his way into a hotel to park his rented car in the lobby. Now, Roger and Pete Townshend will return to a hero's welcome 36 years later.

Back in London an invitation was being posted to Roger to attend the Capital FM Music Awards and accept the Outstanding

Contribution to Music Award on behalf of The Who. Roger was to receive a standing ovation as he collected the trophy at the Royal Lancaster Hotel.

Meanwhile, in dozens of countries around the world, The History Channel is showing a programme in which Roger can be seen fashioning a canoe from a fallen tree using a primitive chisel of the kind employed by frontiersmen in North America 200 years ago. For Roger is the presenter of *Extreme History*, a series which examines survival techniques of years ago. Chipping away at the log reminds him, he tells viewers, of how he made his first guitar from a block of wood, hopelessly unable to afford the real thing. That was a memory trawled up from all of 48 years ago, when he was a 12-year-old and, like countless others, had excitedly caught the early strains of Elvis Presley and Buddy Holly on the radio.

The man who famously sang the words 'Hope I die before I get old' turned 60 in March 2004. Pete Townshend, the man who wrote those lyrics for rock's classic in-your-face anthem 'My Generation', will reach the same milestone in May 2005. The irony of those lyrics is not lost on either of them.

Roger is in every way a survivor. His very birth was something of a miracle, his mother having been advised she could never have children. As a child he came chillingly close to dying of a poisoned stomach, but pulled through. As a young man and in middle age he somehow came safely through the madness, the chaos and the excesses that went with being on the road as lead singer in what was arguably the greatest, and certainly the most riotous and destructive, rock 'n' roll band in the world. He survived.

'Being lead singer of The Who is a very physical job that keeps me in shape,' he explains, 'but even way back in the early days, I kept things pretty clean. Don't get me wrong, I had a good time all right, but I was sharing the stage with some raging alcoholics and addicts, and one of us had to keep a clear head.'

Roger has survived witnessing lung cancer claim the lives of both his mother and father, and breast cancer bring his sister's life to an end at the tragically young age of 32. A second sister has also had a brush with cancer, and he has used his own gift of continuing life, health and rock icon status to work with extraordinary dedication to raise huge sums of money to better the lives of teenagers stricken by the disease.

And yet, in addition to his natural survival qualities, there has been more than a hint of Lady Luck throughout his career. It's very doubtful Roger would be the star he is now if he had not been given the chance to transform himself from competent but unexceptional singer of Chicago blues to dramatic interpreter of Pete Townshend's songs. 'Pete was the most important songwriter of the twentieth century,' he concedes gratefully. 'He did more to move music and lyrics on than any other writer. He paints wonderful pictures for me, emotionally and lyrically.'

Where would Roger be now if his bandmates had decided not to reinstate him after they had unanimously kicked him out of The Who after a violent confrontation with Keith Moon? Luck and timing decreed that a heavy workload for The Who, and the strong association of Roger's vocals with the then just-breaking 'My Generation', meant he had to be restored as lead singer.

Would Roger and The Who have been the worldwide sensation they became had the sun not picked its moment to steal so magically over the horizon, bathing him in a golden glow, just as he sang the inspiring refrain from 'Tommy' See Me, Feel Me, Touch Me, Heal Me during the peace-and-love rock festival at Woodstock? It was extraordinarily fortunate timing – the band should have been on stage many hours earlier.

'It was like a gift from God,' says Roger of that mystical moment, captured so memorably and so tellingly in the Woodstock movies screened around the world. For many it was and still is the highlight of the festival. For The Who it was a gargantuan moment, and within a year Roger and the rest of the group were all millionaires.

But for providence and, it must be said, a steely determination to follow his dream of becoming a rock singer, Roger believes he might have been a teenage delinquent headed for a life of petty crime and villainy like some of the rough crowd he had rubbed shoulders with for teenage kicks. Rock 'n' roll, he willingly admits, offered him a different life, a way out from the tedium of factory work.

Rock music is littered with ex-wives who have fallen by the wayside, casualties of the hedonistic lifestyle that accompanies elevation of their husbands to the status of rock gods. Roger would never call himself a saint, but his marriage to former model Heather remains rock solid after more than 30 years, their children the focal point of their lives.

If Roger's solo recording efforts have not been as successful as he might have hoped, his voice continues to inspire new generations through the continuing sale in vast quantities of CDs by The Who.

Recently, while looking back nostalgically over the past four decades, he still marvelled at how The Who managed to become quite so special. 'How come four people who were different and didn't socialise came together and made music with such passion?' he wondered. 'I really appreciate what we had between us. For four people to get together and create something like that is a magical thing. I mean, there's billions of people on the planet. Why did us four come together and make that noise?'

That noise, as he tongue-in-cheek describes it, has brought him wealth beyond his wildest dreams, the pride in achievement of a man from such humble beginnings, satisfaction in ambitions realised and a place in Rock 'n' Roll's Hall of Fame.

For all this and much besides, Roger touchingly admits he is profoundly grateful. 'We have been incredibly lucky. I wake up every morning thinking, Gawd, what a life! When you think about the great bands of all time, there's only a handful like the Stones and The Who who've gone on for as long as we have. And you think, why us? It's an extraordinary life we've had. Why should we come together and make that noise and create that extraordinary thing? God knows. Life is weird.'

CHAPTER ONE

BORN SURVIVOR

He was a miracle baby, and I was a miracle mother. I couldn't believe it when I first held Roger in my arms.

Irene Daltrey

The most remarkable thing about the birth of Roger Daltrey was that it ever happened at all. If his mother, Irene, had been a less courageous, less determined woman and had listened to the frequently repeated medical advice that with her fragile constitution she should not even contemplate the dangerous business of getting pregnant and starting a family, her son would never have entered the world.

Harry Daltrey married his pretty, auburn-haired sweetheart Irene in 1936. The Second World War was still three years away and unthinkable at that time, when Hitler was just a slightly comical German leader left fuming as American Jesse Owens soured the Aryan dream by scooping gold medals at the Berlin Olympics. Harry and Irene were both 23 and the two Londoners had been courting for several years before tying the knot.

But the happiness of the London couple was rudely interrupted just nine months after the wedding, when Irene was struck down with a kidney disease that was to blight her life for the next nine years and apparently dash for ever her hopes of having children. In hospital doctors removed one of her kidneys, but then she contracted polyneuritis, an inflammation of the nerves, which in turn led to a form of polio. 'I was put in an iron lung for two months and I really thought it was the end, that I was going to die,' Irene recounted years later. 'I was completely paralysed. All the feeling left my body, and I lay in Seagrave Road Fever Hospital just staring at the ceiling for a whole year. I had no feeling anywhere. Then came five years in a wheelchair. I felt so helpless, and hopeless too.' Sadly, Irene was never to regain full use of her hands.

Irene's despair was only increased when all her doctors told her that becoming a mother with just one kidney was out of the question. Forget it, they told her, it won't ever happen – a shattering verdict for a newly married woman in her early twenties. To add to Irene's heartbreak, her four sisters were all busy starting families and she dreaded the thought of being the only one to end up childless.

When the Second World War started, Harry was drafted into the army. However, on several occasions he was granted compassionate leave because of Irene's ill health, sometimes of up to three months, and during one of their reunions she surprised everyone by becoming pregnant.

Irene was by now in her thirties, and throughout those distressing five years in a wheelchair and the years that followed, she had never given up hope. She had always wanted a baby and resolutely clung to the belief that one day she would succeed in giving birth. 'And then it happened!' she said. 'I knew it was a gamble. But when I became pregnant in 1943 I was determined to go through with it, despite all the warnings.'

Inevitably there was many an anxious moment in the months leading up to the birth. Harry was away in Germany fighting in the war and years of illness had taken its toll on Irene. But her courage was buoyed by the support of various relatives and friends who regularly visited her at the couple's rented home at 15 Percy Road, Shepherd's Bush, west London.

Those winter months of 1943–4 saw a relentless effort by the Nazi war machine to bomb London into submission, and the end of February 1944 found a heavily pregnant Irene regularly hurrying as fast as she could to leave the house and take shelter in the bowels of Shepherd's Bush Tube station after a wailing siren signalled yet another German air raid was on its way. Each time she sought refuge, Irene took with her some meagre provisions and some blankets to stave off the bitter cold as she desperately tried to snatch some much-needed sleep. On one occasion she left her home not a moment too soon, because the house next door suffered a direct hit and was reduced to a pile of rubble. The bombing killed 20 people, but somehow the Daltreys' home escaped serious damage and remained habitable.

Huddling together for warmth with other local residents on the station platform, Irene could hear the muffled rumble of bombs exploding in the vicinity about a hundred feet above her. It was at this moment that Roger Daltrey started to indicate he was ready to make his arrival in the world. Irene knew at once that her baby was on its way and the wardens helped her to climb the stairs up to the street. 'We were all scared stiff,' said Irene, who never forgot the horror of emerging from underground to be greeted by the sight of almost every house in Percy Road ablaze from the relentless assault from the sky. 'An ambulance rushed me to the hospital through the smoke. Our street had been hit. Twenty were killed that night. Even then Roger kept me waiting for a full week.'

The previous nine years of ill health inevitably made for a difficult birth. At one point it looked as though Irene's child would be a Leap Year baby, born on 29 February 1944, and she begged the hospital to delay delivery, if possible, until 1 March 1944. She told the nurses she wanted to hang on until then because that date happened to be her mother's birthday. Irene got her wish, by just a couple of hours.

Finally Roger Harry Daltrey was safely delivered at 2am at

Hammersmith Hospital, in Du Cane Road, not far from Wormwood Scrubs Prison, on 1 March 1944. For Irene, it was a moment of overwhelming joy when she came round to hear a smiling nurse inform her: 'You've got a lovely boy.'

When she had first gone into labour Irene had been frightened that the terrible scare she had suffered from the bombs might have somehow harmed or even disfigured her baby. Weak and exhausted as she was, she knew it was the happiest moment of her life. 'A miracle. He was a miracle baby, and I was a miracle mother,' she said. 'I couldn't believe it when I first held Roger in my arms.' Irene had the admiration of family, friends and medical staff, all fully aware of the ordeal she had been through to become a mother. Having triumphed against all the odds, she dressed Roger in pristine white for the first two years of his life.

Irene's immense relief and her pride and joy at defying medical opinion were rapidly tempered by Harry's having to kiss his wife and new-born son a tearful goodbye shortly afterwards. He had been given compassionate leave to be with Irene for the birth, but now he was returning to Germany to stand shoulder to shoulder once more with his fellow gunners in the Royal Artillery. As the war raged on with no sign of ending, Irene was just one of many thousands of wives of British servicemen fearful that she would end up widowed. Now she had her longed-for baby, she worried that he might never get the chance to know his father.

Within weeks of Roger's arrival, Prime Minister Winston Churchill was ominously warning the British nation: 'The hour of our greatest effort is approaching.' Londoners braced themselves for another blitz, and now the capital's residents were threatened with a new peril as Hitler unleashed Germany's much-vaunted 'secret weapon' the V-1 flying bomb, a pilotless, jet-propelled aircraft capable of flying at 400mph and carrying nearly a ton of explosive.

By 11 July 1944, Churchill was telling a sombre House of Commons that between 100 and 150 'doodlebugs' or 'buzz bombs,' as the missiles became known, were being launched against Britain every day, and a total of 2,754 of them had caused 2,752 deaths and 8,000 casualties.

The very real terror and the rising casualty toll as the Germans intensified their doodlebug attacks prompted the second mass wartime exodus of children from London. More than 41,000 mothers and children were evacuated, among them Irene and the infant Roger. Their destination was a farm in Stranraer, on the south-west coast of Scotland, so remote that the nearest village shop was several miles away. It was to be Irene and Roger's home for the next 13 months, but after the warmth of London it felt like living on another planet, for it was so isolated and inaccessible a retreat that mother and son barely saw another soul during the entire time they were there.

Irene was still having difficulty in walking and using her hands, which compounded her problems, especially in the snow, and there were no neighbours to help her out. Water had to be collected in a bucket from a tap a ten-minute walk away, there was no electric lighting, only oil lamps, and because oil for these was in short supply there was no alternative for Irene but to go to bed when darkness fell.

Worse still, there were no proper cooking facilities. What little food Irene managed to find had to be cooked over an open fire in the hearth. She was desperately worried that Roger would not survive such hardship, and the fact that all she could feed him every day was boiled potatoes led to a brush with rickets. It was a desperate struggle in every way for Irene and her undernourished baby, especially as she was unused to living in the country.

But at least the farm was a safe haven, and indeed Irene and Roger had left the capital in the nick of time. By 9 September 1944 a second Battle of London was being fought, with Chiswick, not far from the Shepherd's Bush area, where Irene and Harry had always lived, the first to feel the force of a new and terrible German weapon. The V-2 long-range rocket, weighing 15 tons and carrying a one-ton warhead, was launched from the Netherlands and Germany. These missiles gave no warning save for a 'tearing sound, like an express train' as they landed vertically from a high altitude, travelling faster than the speed of sound. When the first one landed in Chiswick it caused a blast wave that could be felt not just in Percy Road but much further.

But then, on 13 May 1945, suddenly the war was over, and Irene and Roger were able to return to their home in London. Irene and other relations and friends of the Daltreys laid on a big party for Harry's homecoming, and he returned proudly wearing a lance corporal's stripe on his sleeve. 'That was my very first memory – of my dad coming back from the war in his tin helmet,' Roger recalled later. Irene's recollection was the look of disgust on her little son's face when he saw this man, a stranger to Roger, getting into bed with his mother.

From his early childhood Roger was always getting up to some sort of mischief. When he was three his parents were alarmed to discover that he had managed to swallow a large nail, which required hospital surgeons to open him up to effect an extraction. Young Roger emerged from surgery with a lasting reminder, a sizeable scar on his body. Years later, when he ran with a rough crowd in Shepherd's Bush and needed to show what a tough nut he was, he would pull up his shirt and imaginatively brag that the scar was the legacy of a fight with a thug who had pulled out a knife and stabbed him.

Unfortunately for Roger, the extraction of the nail was not the end of the matter. The nail had been riddled with rust and over time it harmed the lining of Roger's stomach. By the time he was five he had developed an ulcer which brought him close to death. The poison had spread through his stomach, making him seriously ill.

'We almost lost him,' Harry recalled. 'He was back inside West London hospital for six weeks while they fought for his life.' Irene was distraught. Having overcome huge odds to give birth, she now faced the heartbreaking prospect of losing her little son because of a rusty nail. But Roger showed a strength, a resilience and an instinct for survival that would be a hallmark of his character throughout his life, and he pulled through.

When he was sufficiently recovered, Roger went first to Westfield Road Infants' School and later to Victoria Primary School, both near Shepherd's Bush. Harry and Irene, heartened to find that Roger's reports invariably showed he was doing well at art, music and PT, also made sure their son went to Sunday school. They hoped he might join the choir there, as he had started to show a real interest in music and had begun to enjoy trying to pick out a few tunes on an old piano at home. But young Roger was not taken with the idea of becoming a choirboy. He did, however, take up the trumpet when he joined the Boys' Brigade, where he also liked to exercise in the gym, which helped put some muscles on his wiry frame.

Having safely produced Roger, Irene went on to prove the doctors wrong twice more by giving birth to two sisters for her son: Gillian, born two years later, and Carol, born 12 months after her in 1947. The Daltreys were a staunchly working-class, tightly knit family but, like many families living in post-war London, they found there was peace but not prosperity. Harry, who had left school at 14, worked as an insurance clerk and later as a clerk for Armitage Shanks in Acton, a company which made bathroom furniture, water closets and sanitary fittings – a job which later earned him a nickname from Roger as 'the lavvy man'. Money was not exactly plentiful and although for a long time he couldn't afford a car, Harry eventually managed to scrape together the cash to buy an old London taxi, which was spacious enough to take the family plus assorted uncles and aunts for holidays at Jaywick, near Clacton in Essex. There was much merriment among the occupants when Harry lowered the cab's hood and they drove around pretending they were royalty.

The house in Percy Road was usually bursting with various

members of the Daltrey clan because Irene had eight brothers and sisters, and the three-storey building was rented not just by Harry and Irene but also by one of Roger's many aunts. The house was conveniently divided diagonally so that the aunt occupied the three rooms downstairs and a room at the back upstairs. A further four rooms upstairs were occupied by Harry and Irene and their children. Since the aunt also had three daughters and Roger had two sisters, the future frontman of The Who grew up surrounded by females. If he got fed up with their girly chatter he would take himself off to play football or cricket at the local bombsites or in the streets with some of the many other young lads who lived in his street.

Early on in his life Roger developed a fondness for fishing. 'I always loved it as a kid,' he says. 'Gravel pits, ponds or even the Grand Union Canal, which, believe it or not, is a great place to fish. You don't just catch bike frames and old boots.'

Roger was generally a happy young boy who willingly accepted the fairly structured working-class family life of Saturday-morning films at the local cinema in Shepherd's Bush, a visit to gran down the road at weekends and Sunday school and church on Sundays. But in the tough environment of Shepherd's Bush he had to learn to look after himself, especially as he regularly got picked on by boys bigger than him who liked to poke fun at his bow legs. They soon discovered, though, that Roger was prepared to stand up for himself and could throw a punch or two when required.

Roger was 11 years old when a song called '(We're Gonna) Rock Around the Clock' by the American Bill Haley and the Comets created a dividing line between all popular songs that had gone before and all that followed. It was the beginning of the rock era. The year was 1955 and 'Rock Around the Clock' was first heard under the opening credits of *The Blackboard Jungle*, a movie starring Glenn Ford as a high-school teacher confronted by violent students.

As in America, the film's confrontational content inspired riots in British cinemas and it was denounced as degenerate. But 'Rock Around the Clock', which blended a country sound with rhythm and blues, created a sensation and went on to top the British 'hit parade', as the charts were then called, for six weeks spanning the end of 1955 and the beginning of 1956. The song was rock music's opening salvo and ranks as one of the most significant recordings in popular music history. In Britain it ushered in a new kind of sound unfamiliar to listeners to the BBC's main entertainment radio station, the staid Light Programme. Up until then the brass section in *The Billy Cotton Bandshow* was about as exciting as live music ever got on the BBC's radio output.

The following year Bill Haley brought his Comets to London, drove audiences wild and repeatedly exhorted youngsters like Roger to 'Shake, Rattle and Roll' and to 'Razzle Dazzle' to his infectious beat. It was that same year, 1957, that Elvis Presley was also famously taking his hip-swivelling walk down lonely street to 'Heartbreak Hotel' and Lonnie Donegan was nasally extolling the virtues of that mighty fine line the 'Rock Island Line'. Bill Haley was the first rock pioneer, but it was 'Elvis the Pelvis', America's King of Rock 'n' Roll, and then Britain's King of Skiffle Lonnie who made an indelible impression on young Roger. To him their music, the driving beat at the heart of the fifties, was like a clarion call to be a singer. 'From the time I heard Elvis Presley and Lonnie Donegan, I didn't want to be anything else,' said Roger who, 47 years later, showed he meant what he said when he was only too happy to appear at the Royal Albert Hall in London in a tribute concert to Donegan.

It was also in 1957 that Harry and Irene were intrigued to find Roger staggering home from school one afternoon carrying a large block of wood. 'What are you going to do with that, son?' Harry enquired. 'I'm going to make a guitar,' came the indignant reply. Roger had often paused to gaze longingly at the guitars on display in a nearby music shop as he made his way home from school. He would press his face up to the window to examine the price tags

9

hanging from the necks of the shiny instruments in the vain hope that they might be financially in reach. But the then quite revolutionary Fender Stratocaster guitar, much favoured by Buddy Holly at the time, cost as much as £125 as early as 1954, a price way beyond the reach of someone of Roger's age. So he resigned himself to the fact that the only way he was ever going to own a guitar was by making one for himself. His DIY approach was not quite as overambitious as it might first appear. The skiffle craze which was sweeping the country in the mid-1950s enabled anybody with a tea chest and a broom handle, or a washboard, plus a sense of rhythm, to get up and perform popular songs. To Roger, building his own guitar was a sensible extension of that do-it-yourself musical mentality.

Diligently, he set about fashioning his guitar with whatever tools he could lay his hands on. The covetous gaze he regularly cast at the brightly coloured Gibsons, Gretschs and Strats, tantalisingly gleaming at him in the music shop window, began to take on a more practical purpose when he took to keeping a ruler with him so he could hold it up to the window and correctly gauge the measurements of the frets, the neck and the bodies of the guitars he wanted to copy. Using bits of wood, metal and string, Roger eventually proudly produced his first painstakingly made primitive guitar, which at least looked like the real thing after he had taken it down to an uncle's shop to have it french-polished and painted.

Before long Roger had taught himself a few chords and was showing a steely determination to improve. He taught himself new tunes by ear and was quick to ask others for advice and help in shaping new chords and learning chord progressions. He spent hours on end tucked away in his bedroom at the back of the house strumming away.

Harry and Irene first got an inkling that his interest in the guitar really might lead on to bigger things when they took the family to Brighton for a seaside holiday. Naturally, Roger's beloved home-made guitar went with him. One evening his parents were taking a leisurely stroll along the promenade when they noticed a commotion on the beach. A sizeable crowd had gathered and Harry and Irene immediately thought that maybe someone had been pulled out of the sea after getting into difficulties or there had been some sort of accident. But as they drew nearer they saw it was Roger at the centre of the hubbub. He was sitting cross-legged on the beach surrounded by teenagers dancing to his strumming and singing. Eventually, Roger was moved on by the police after a cursory ticking-off. Two years later Harry further encouraged Roger to pursue what appeared to be his main interest in life by buying him an Epiphone, his first proper guitar.

In 1957, when Roger was 13, Harry and Irene moved the Daltrey family to 135 Fielding Road in Bedford Park, where they were now able to afford to rent the whole house. Little did they know then that their son, soon to be strumming away on his rough-hewn guitar with a first group he had formed called the Detours, would, 15 years later, be a rock star wealthy enough to buy that house outright for them for £4,000 and furnish it with every domestic luxury.

Although it was a modest house, with a small upstairs back bedroom given over to Roger, the move was definitely upmarket. It was only a couple of miles west of their previous home but Bedford Park was a much more salubrious area than Shepherd's Bush. Crossing the social divide was not, however, much to Roger's liking after the natural working-class chumminess of the folk he knew around 'the Bush'. Until then he was not even aware there was such a thing as a social divide. It forcibly hit home when, after passing his 11-plus examination, which marked him out as one of the brighter boys to be channelled through the English state-school system, he went on to Acton County Grammar School in Gunnersbury Lane, near Acton Town station. The school's intake was largely middle-class pupils from leafy, tree-lined and affluent Bedford Park and Ealing.

'I used to love going to school in Shepherd's Bush,' said Roger. 'I loved the teachers, it was like one big happy family and everyone talked the same. When I got to grammar school it was horrendous, like being thrown to the lions. I felt totally out of place. They even sang in different accents. I met my first posh accent and I immediately got a terrible complex. I just didn't fit in.' He added tellingly: 'Where I came from, I didn't know people like I met at Acton County. I thought everybody talked like me – until I got there. I loved rock 'n' roll because they hated it.'

Moving school meant Roger lost touch with most of his pals, and the thought of having to conform at the grammar school filled with pupils who largely seemed to speak with plums in their mouths brought out the worst in him.

'I'd never met people who talked like that before,' he said. 'I felt so isolated. So I became a rebel. I was a very violent character then as well. Where I used to live, you had to be a hard nut. If anybody offered you outside for a punch-up, you had to go, and you had to have a good fight.'

Roger's readiness to let his fists do the talking for him was partly due to his insecurity over his lack of stature. Neither Irene nor Harry was tall and Roger often found he was quite a bit smaller than other boys of his age. He may have preferred settling arguments with his knuckles but insisted: 'I never went looking for trouble. I never hurt anybody for the sake of it, but I could look after myself. I never ended up in hospital over a beating, although I had some pretty large lumps.'

Right from day one at Acton County, Roger was trouble, and swiftly marked down as a disruptive pupil. 'Anything that went wrong, it was Roger Daltrey that got the blame,' recalled school caretaker Alfred McMahon. Roger concedes that 'Mac', as he was known around the school, was not far wrong. 'I was totally anti-everything,' he said. 'I was a right bastard, a hard nut. I must have been a nightmare for my parents. I just totally closed the doors to ever wanting to know what they had to teach me. Rock 'n' roll was the only thing I ever wanted to get into.'

Something Roger did get into in a big way at school was mischief – at every opportunity. Instead of turning up in the uniform of grey flannels and blue blazer, Roger presented himself in Teddy-boy outfit of drainpipe trousers, bum-freezer jacket, winklepicker shoes and a bootlace tie he made himself by cutting his school tie in half. 'He stood out like a canary among a lot of blackbirds,' said Mac. But Roger didn't care. By now he was cultivating his fair hair so that it swept upwards into a fashionable Elvis and Teddy-boy quiff and tapered off at the back in a 'duck's arse' (euphemistically known in polite circles as a 'DA' to avoid the uttering of what was considered a dirty phrase). John Entwistle, later to join Roger as a bass guitarist in his Detours, remembers sitting near him at school assembly and 'looking straight into this Tony Curtis-style pompadour'.

Roger certainly stood out among the other, smartly dressed pupils. 'I decided I was going to be me, whatever the price,' he said. 'So I got myself pink socks, green trousers and a Teddy-boy jacket with about five pockets going up the side.' This garish garb, which contrasted vibrantly with the other boys' clothes, made him feel cock of the walk. He had the threads, he talked the talk very much his way, and he walked the walk, often menacingly.

Very soon teachers were complaining not just about Roger's appearance but also about his attitude, not least his constantly distracting other pupils in lessons by loudly humming hits by the first wave of American rockers, like Presley, Jerry Lee Lewis, Eddie Cochran and Buddy Holly. These were now Roger's heroes and he found he couldn't get their hits out of his brain. It wasn't just the melody or the guitar work: he admired what they said in their lyrics and how they said it.

Roger told one of the authors years later: 'Music to me is all about people out there who can't articulate their feelings very well. It's great to find something in music and go, "Blimey, that's just how I feel." That's how it was for me in the old days with Buddy Holly. Why I liked him was that he was singing about things I thought about, but he could say it a lot better than I could.'

The huge impression the hits of the day made on Roger at that time cannot be overemphasised. Some 20 years later, when he was the castaway on the popular BBC Radio programme *Desert Island Discs*, Roger listed Larry Williams's 'Short Fat Fanny' (1957), Jerry Lee Lewis's 'Great Balls of Fire' (1957), Buddy Holly's 'Rave On' (1958), the Big Bopper's 'Chantilly Lace' (1958) and Eddie Cochran's 'C'Mon Everybody' (1959) among his all-time favourites.

Roger can still vividly remember a pivotal encounter with a teacher at Acton County who embodied everything he hated in the older generation. Roger was 14 at the time and had come to school brimming with enthusiasm for Elvis Presley, whom he had seen on television the night before. Watching Elvis, with his slicked-back hair, guitar slung round his neck and girls screaming at his gyrating hips, more than ever convinced young Roger that he too was going to get into rock music big time. Elvis was the perfect teenage idol – rebellious, a rule-breaker, a young man who got up the noses of his parents' generation. To teenagers who had grown up in post-war Britain with the austerity of ration books, Elvis with his Memphis mansion and fleet of gleaming Cadillacs was the King who had made it big through rock 'n' roll.

Next day in class Roger couldn't contain his enthusiasm for Elvis and asked his teacher what he thought of him. 'He's disgusting,' came the sneering reply, which left Roger feeling crushed. 'That was one of my teachers at Acton Grammar School, and I guess he was only about 30 at the time,' Roger could still recount with feeling in an interview 40 years later, so vivid was the memory of this damning put-down. 'But his attitude was old. He was already dead as far as I was concerned. I hated him and everything he stood for. He and his kind were just training people for a life with a briefcase. Give me Elvis any day, I thought to myself. At least he's free.'

Before long Roger extended his struggle against authority by secretly setting himself up as the school bookie, even flaunting his self-appointed position by going around taking bets from other pupils with a satchel over his shoulder marked 'Honest Joe'. On a small scale it occasionally proved a lucrative venture for him until the fateful 1961 running at Epsom of Britain's premier flat race, the Derby. One boy elected to place the then princely sum of two shillings (10p in today's money) on a horse called Psidium. To the general dismay of bookies around the country, and in particular to Honest Joe of Acton County Grammar School, French jockey Roger Poincelet sensationally brought Psidium first past the winning post at the remarkable odds of 66-1.

True to his Honest Joe moniker, Roger paid out, albeit reluctantly, and a jubilant grammar school boy went home with his pockets weighed down with his unexpected winnings. Inevitably, there was an inquest after the boy's mother marched up to the school demanding to know how her flush son had come by such a large amount of money.

Roger's toll of misbehaviour with other bad boys in the school encompassed smoking, using milk bottles as skittles, filching lavatory chains and creeping into the school hall at night to paint all the lightbulbs bright red.

Mac the caretaker would turn a blind eye to the lesser pranks, but two major misdemeanours involving Roger infuriated the headmaster, Desmond Kibblewhite. The first was on April Fool's Day, when the head happened to be addressing the school. At the end of his speech the sound of a lavatory being flushed echoed around the school assembly hall from the amplified speakers.

The second transgression which irked Mr Kibblewhite came after he had mockingly labelled the school's troublemakers 'the Cuds'. This term derived from 'chewing the cud', ruminant animals' habit of chewing food over and over again. The Cuds, the head explained to his staff, were those pupils who had to have rules and facts repeated over and over again before they were able to grasp them.

One cloudless summer afternoon Mr Kibblewhite was walking around the playing field during a school cricket match when three boys hiding behind the sightscreen suddenly flung a banner over the top of it. 'The Cuds Is Coming,' it proclaimed – a take-off of the slogan 'The Birds Is Coming', which at the time was being heavily used on advertising hoardings to promote Alfred Hitchcock's latest chilling movie, *The Birds*. Behind the impudent banner on the cricket field were three boys – Roger Daltrey and two pupils in the year below him, Peter Townshend and John Entwistle. It would not be the last time the three of them would cause a stir.

Mr Kibblewhite summed up Roger with schoolmasterly precision but little warmth: 'He was a misfit. He was no good in school. Daltrey was a very mixed-up kid. It was an accumulation of troubles, really. He was a curious mixture of love-hate. He wasn't dim. He was a normal 11-plus entry to the grammar school. But his social background was like a millstone around his neck. Social pressures proved too much for him.'

Having seen Roger pass his 11-plus examination with top grades, Irene and Harry hoped fervently that Roger would go on to university. At the age of 11 it seemed a realistic possibility – there was in 1955 no hint of the trouble to come. His school report for most subjects, including 'The Choir' and 'Boxing', glowed with praise like 'V. Good' or Excellent'. It went on to describe him as 'intelligent, eager, helpful and co-operative'.

But Roger's view of school rapidly became so jaundiced that he was never going to build on his impressive grades. 'Shakespeare was like having a tooth pulled,' he would laugh years later when taking a role in a BBC production of *The Comedy of Errors*. Back then, however, all too often he would come home from school muttering darkly that the headmaster always seemed to be picking on him.

Eventually Roger's parents sought a meeting with Mr Kibblewhite, who told them: 'If you have 500 boys here all in navy-blue macs and then one turns up in a white mac, it's so out-standing. That's Roger.' It came as a surprise to Irene, who always watched her son leave the house in the morning smartly dressed in his uniform. But, as she quickly realised, Roger was like countless other schoolboys who nipped around the corner, tore off their caps and ties and stuffed them in their pockets as soon as they were out of sight of home.

By the time Roger was 15, Mr Kibblewhite's patience had finally expired. Having endured a hard year of almost constant confronta-tion with young Daltrey, including the teenager turning up for a school photo in his full Teddy-boy outfit, he advised Irene and Harry that, as their son seemed to have no interest in school what-soever, it would be better for all concerned if he left. 'All he's interested in is music, music, music, nothing else,' the exasperated head told Roger's parents.

Finally Roger was caught smoking once again and it was the last straw. Mr Kibblewhite explained: 'Roger was a lively lad. We had a year of confrontation. He was out of place, uncomfortable. There's no rationalisation to what kids will do when they feel society's against them. There was nothing really criminal about it. But if a boy is caught with stolen lavatory chains in his pocket then one has to do something about it.'

So, in 1959, Roger was expelled from Acton County Grammar School after being interviewed by the school governors as part of a formal suspension procedure. He then had a final meeting with Mr Kibblewhite during which the headmaster made one last effort to get to the bottom of his troubles. 'What's the matter with you, Roger?' he asked. Roger, by now noticeably shaking a little as the gravity of his expulsion sank in, misunderstood Mr Kibblewhite's line of questioning and replied: 'It must be my nerves, sir.'

Roger's expulsion came as a terrible shock and disappointment to his parents. Their son was emerging into adulthood branded as a troublemaker, a grammar school dropout, a misfit and a rebel-lious loner. Worse still, he was gaining a reputation locally as an aggressive teenager who was all too ready with his fists. 'He was a right little bully, the world's worst,' said his sister Gillian.

Many years later Roger often looked back, ruing that he had been sent to a school he positively hated. He would have loved to learn another language, to write better and read more. 'I've regretted all my life that no one sat down with me and explained that school is for yourself, not anyone else. I used to find myself in school thinking, what the hell have I done to deserve this? The working-class attitude then was: "You've got to pass your 11-plus." Well, I passed with flying colours, but then what? I didn't get a reward. I was sent to a school I hated. It's a shame.'

Harry and Irene were not the sort of parents to allow their son just to become an idle layabout once his school days were over. They had lived through a terrible war and life was not for wasting. Besides, Roger wasn't interested in simply doing nothing. He was by now playing guitar in pubs for ten shillings (50p) an hour pocket money and he wanted a daytime job because he needed money to buy clothes and take out girlfriends. Soon he started working part-time on a building site in Shepherd's Bush as an electrician's mate.

Roger's first rate of pay was one shilling (5p) an hour – around the time that Harold Macmillan, Eton-educated Conservative Prime Minister told the country: 'You've never had it so good.' Roger stuck at the job for just six weeks, his head still full of notions that his future lay in rock 'n' roll. One day, he promised himself, it would make him rich and famous.

'If you come from the streets, you've got how many ways out?' he said later. 'You can either work in a factory and become an ordinary geezer. Or if you've got any spark of wanting to be a total individual, you can become one of four things – a footballer, a boxer, a criminal or a pop singer. I guess that's why I'll still be rockin' in my wheelchair. Rock 'n' roll was my saviour.'

CHAPTER TWO

Do You Wanna be in My band?

The greatest bloody triumph of my school days was when Roger asked me if I could play guitar. If he had ever said: 'Come out in the playground and I'll fight you', I would have been down in one punch. Music was the only way I could ever win.

Pete Townshend

Roger Daltrey left Acton County Grammar School under the blackest of clouds and with a myriad of miserable memories. But at least he has the school to thank for his first introduction to two musically like-minded pupils, John Entwistle and Pete Townshend.

John and Pete were both in the year below Roger and would not become proper members of his band the Detours until after Roger had left the school. But later, when he was casting around for musicians to augment and improve his band, it was important to him that he was familiar with both from his school days. Roger had little difficulty in remembering Pete. The two of them discovered their shared musical interest during a playground ruck when Pete yelled: 'Mind my fingers, I play guitar' and Roger said: 'So do I.'

Roger marked Pete down, as he later described him, as 'a nose on a stick' – not the most sensitive description of a lad who was regularly teased and taunted at school about the size of his nose. 'When I was a kid,' Pete told the *Evening Standard* years later, 'I had this enormous great hooter and I was always being baited about it. So I used to think: I'll bloody well show them. I'll push this huge hooter at them from every newspaper in England. Then they won't laugh at me.'

Unlike a lot of embryonic groups formed by young lads in their early teens at that time, the Detours were a real working band, even while Roger was still at Acton County. While other groups spent the majority of their time learning new numbers, practising or simply playing for their own amusement or to impress friends, the Detours were different. Roger took his band seriously – he had to because they went out and played for cash. They had bookings at venues ranging from private parties to local working men's clubs and small dance halls, and he knew how quickly word would get around if the Detours didn't come up to scratch in their performances.

Roger was determined to set decent standards at gigs and in turn he relished the reward of cash pressed into his hand at the end of every date. 'I always knew I'd make it after starting the Detours,' he said. 'We never started for any reason, just that we liked playing together. We had no great ambition or anything. But every week we used to get that much better.'

In those early days Roger led the Detours as lead guitarist and was backed by a changing personnel who variously sat in on drums, bass and vocals. Eventually a boy named Colin Dawson clinched the regular job of singer. There was also Reg Bowen, a rhythm guitarist whose limited ability on the instrument Roger tolerated because of a priceless asset: very conveniently, Reg's parents were prepared to let the Detours rehearse at their home.

The second ingredient in the revolutionary musical mix that was to explode as The Who arrived after Roger spotted John Entwistle walking home one night carrying a home-made bass guitar. Like Roger, John had been unable to afford the real thing and had made his own very basic model from a lump of mahogany with the help of a carpenter who shaped it for him. 'I hear you play bass?' Roger asked – somewhat unnecessarily, John thought, since he was obviously clutching that very instrument.

Roger then asked John if he'd like to come along the following night to a Detours rehearsal in Shepherd's Bush. John duly turned up, and when Roger later asked him: 'Do you think we're any good?' he nodded and agreed to join. It meant John leaving the Scorpions, which also featured his pal Pete Townshend, but he was prepared to switch to the Detours. At first John was wary of Roger as he remembered him from school as big bad Roger, leader of the Teds. But, by joining Roger in the Detours, he could content himself with the knowledge that at least he was now in a band which would actually get paid for playing gigs.

Like Roger, John Alec Entwistle had been born during the Blitz. But unlike Roger, John had real musical pedigree by the time he joined the Detours. He had been proficient enough on the trumpet to be the only boy at Acton County to earn selection for the Middlesex Youth Orchestra, whose members were culled from the most promising musicians in London schools. John's musicianship was later good enough for him to alternate the trumpet with playing the French horn in the orchestra when required.

Outside of school, John had also played in trad jazz bands, one of which was called the Confederates and included Pete Townshend on banjo. It was after this that the two had moved on to join the Scorpions. John's original interest in the bass guitar had been inspired by Duane Eddy, an American who had made the instrument fashionable with a string of solo hits without the benefit of vocals, notably 'The Peter Gunn Theme', 'Because They're Young' and 'Dance with the Guitar Man'. Duane Eddy was in effect rock 'n' roll's first guitar hero, and his simple but resonant guitar playing, allied to a studio production which utilised echo and tape delay, intensified the melodies he twanged on his bass guitar. After hearing Eddy's 'The Twang's the Thang!', John Entwistle needed no second invitation to pluck away at an electric bass.

Like Roger, on leaving school John got himself a job while continuing to play in the evening with the Detours. He worked at the local Inland Revenue office, first as a counter clerk dealing with members of the public who came in to query their tax bills and later as a filing clerk. John would keep his job until the release of The Who's first record, 'I Can't Explain', in January 1965 finally prompted him to pack it in.

As a fully-fledged and musically capable member of the Detours, John didn't take long to cotton on that Reg Bowen had his limitations on rhythm guitar. Soon he began suggesting to Roger that Pete Townshend, his old school pal and former bandmate from the Confederates and the Scorpions, should replace Reg.

Peter Dennis Blandford Townshend, a year younger than Roger, came from a family steeped in music and, when The Who turned fully professional, Pete would become the third generation in the Townshend family to choose to make a living from music. Pete's grandfather Horace had been a star of the Jack Shepherd Concert Revue between the wars, and Pete's father, Cliff, played the saxophone with the RAF Dance Orchestra. When the Second World War was over, the orchestra became a hugely popular dance band called the Squadronaires, performing to enthusiastic audiences on the dance-hall circuit and frequently appearing on the radio, on the BBC's Light Programme. Pete's mother, Betty, was also a singer with another dance band, the Sidney Torch Orchestra.

From an early age Pete showed an intention to follow his parents into a career in music. Offered the chance to join the Detours, now working several nights a week, he jumped at it. 'Of all the bands at school, the Detours were the best,' he remembered. 'Roger was the best guitarist, a very basic guitar player but very confident, and very fluid in a way. He could learn something parrot fashion, and then make it very fluid.'

When Pete indicated he was ready to become a Detour, Reg Bowen was summarily tossed out of the band. That caused the immediate problem of having nowhere to practise, so Roger took it upon himself to invite the other members back to his house on nights when he knew his parents would be going out to play cards. The rest of the band would hide around the corner until Roger let them all in once Irene and Harry Daltrey had left the house. Then Roger would order his two younger sisters to bed and swear them to secrecy before setting about rearranging the furniture to accommodate the Detours, their instruments and their sound equipment. Roger knew exactly when his parents would return from their whist drive, and his bandmates had sneaked out of the house and all the furniture was back in its normal place before they stepped through the front door.

Harry and Irene could never understand it when next day their neighbours complained about the racket they'd had to put up with from their house the night before. 'But what do you mean?' Roger's puzzled parents protested. 'How could it have been so noisy? We weren't even here.'

While more than tolerating Roger's avid interest in rock music, Harry and Irene were keen that he should learn a trade. That was the advice generally handed down to working-class teenage boys who left school with few or no qualifications, and it was no different for Roger. After leaving his part-time job on the building site, Roger soon found work not far from home at Chase Products, a sheet-metal factory in Colville Road, south Acton. His idea was to become an apprentice, but he started off as a tea boy. He was sharp enough to realise that if his colleagues wanted five ham rolls, then he could either pop down to the local cafe or sandwich shop and buy them for five shillings or make them up himself for a couple of shillings and turn a profit.

Clive Bowry, who trained Roger on the factory machinery, found Roger a likeable, popular lad. During tea breaks Roger, Clive and their workmates would talk of what they would do if they won the football pools. Roger declared he would go out and buy the best guitars in the world, but he got on well enough with his colleagues to agree with them when they all said they would buy up the factory and work for themselves. Some 22 years later Roger did just that. He invested a five-figure sum in a new firm in Hemel Hempstead called PCD Products, which made racking systems for the computer and electronics industry. And, in a generous and touching gesture to his old pals, he made his former workmates directors.

In his spare moments at the Chase Products factory, Roger set to work making guitars and speaker cabinets for the Detours. 'It must have been the only sheet-metal factory with wood shavings on the floor,' he laughed. 'I used to make all the guitars for the group for the first two years. We literally made all our equipment except the drums.'

With Pete as their latest recruit and Doug Sandom settling in as the regular drummer, the Detours took on a new dimension. Pete proved proficient enough on guitar for Roger occasionally to set aside his guitar to play trombone and John some trumpet. Pete was also able to switch to banjo when necessary. The group's repertoire accordingly became a wide-ranging mix of instrumentals, several trad jazz numbers, some Johnny Cash and American country songs and a smattering of popular ballads. The Detours also covered hit instrumentals by Johnny and the Hurricanes and the John Barry Seven, just two of several groups who regularly hit the charts in those days. The most successful of these outfits were Cliff Richard's backing group, the Shadows, who notched up 12 Top Ten hits from July 1960 to December 1963, including 'Apache', 'Kon-Tiki', 'Wonderful Land', 'Dance On' and 'Foot Tapper', all of which went to number one.

The Detours found their cover versions went down well at their gigs and Shadows numbers, especially, became a regular part of their act. Roger liked to keep his group right up to date with versions of other guitar-based instrumental hits of the day, like 'Walk Don't Run' by the Ventures and the Tornados' worldwide instrumental smash 'Telstar', inspired by the launch of the American communications satellite in 1962. 'We were just doing Top Ten hits and playing for about ten cents,' Roger recalled of the months just before the emergence of the Beatles. 'At the time, the whole thing about groups was a joke.'

The world of showbiz generally was ripe for revolution in 1961. Pop music on the radio in Britain was sparse and there were no licences for commercial stations. There were just three television channels broadcasting only in the evenings, and a typical night's viewing consisted of news, weather and cookery programmes. Elvis Presley and Cliff Richard were chalking up hit after hit, and yet an extraordinarily eclectic mix of records also topped the charts that year. Among these were the novelty number 'Come Outside' by Mike Sarne and Wendy Richard, the storming instrumental 'Nut Rocker' by B Bumble and the Stingers, which was a souped-up version of Tchaikovsky's *Nutcracker Suite*, 'You're Driving Me Crazy', the Temperance Seven dance band's oompah version of a 1930s song, and 'Blue Moon', which featured the vocal gymnastics of the Marcels.

Roger eyed those with chart success enviously. But, however seriously they were taking their music, the Detours were not yet earning enough to be anything more than semi-professional. Pete had enrolled at Ealing Art School, while Roger continued with his job at the factory but lived for the evenings, when he could go home, change his clothes and go out to play a gig with the Detours. Often he would not get back home until the small hours and then have to be up early to go to work. 'I just couldn't wait to get out of that factory,' he said. 'I channelled all my energy and all my frustration into music. Being on stage, doing something I loved, attracted all the girls I wanted, paid for all the beer I could drink and put me a cut above everybody else.'

Meanwhile Doug Sandom worked as a bricklayer, Colin Dawson was a sales rep for a Danish bacon company and John Entwistle continued uneasily with his job at the tax office. Because he had a higher vocal range, John, rather than Roger, was entrusted with singing some of the higher-pitched Beatles numbers, like 'I Saw Her Standing There' and 'Twist and Shout', which were added to the Detours' repertoire once the Fab Four had become famous. After belting out 'Twist and Shout' anything up to five times a night in response to repeated requests, John reported for work each morning with his vocal cords barely functioning. He was very grateful when he was transferred to a new position at the tax office as a filing clerk as he no longer had to say much.

While holding on to their day jobs, by the end of 1962 the Detours were starting to make respectable money as gigs became more frequent. They were playing up to six nights a week at pubs, halls, parties, weddings, barmitzvahs and clubs, with each of them taking home around £12 a week after expenses had been deducted. In Roger's case this matched his earnings at the factory. The plum gig was a regular Sunday-afternoon date playing for American GIs, which realised the then princely sum of £75. That sort of money enabled the boys to buy a van.

Roger was still very much the driving force behind the Detours, in every way. It was Roger who drove the band to gigs in the battered maroon and black van which promoter Bob Druce had provided for them by deducting payments from their weekly earnings. While the rest of the group piled into the back of the van and settled down among the amps and equipment, it was Roger who determinedly sat behind the wheel with his favourite girl of the month sitting in the passenger seat beside him. Painted on the side of the van was the word 'Detours' with a white arrow pointing downwards. Roger liked to drive fast but treated his chauffeur's duties a good deal more conscientiously once he had smashed broadside into the side of a bridge one night, leaving the van with an ugly dent.

It was indirectly Roger's demanding daytime job as a sheet-metal worker that eventually led to his taking over as lead vocalist in the Detours. His fingers were often cut, bruised and raw from his manual work at the factory, and this caused painful problems when forming guitar chords or sliding from fret to fret. Colin Dawson, meanwhile, was earning regular sneering censure from Pete Townshend and John Entwistle for an approach to singing which they felt was more suited to cabaret. On some occasions the singer appeared on stage in a yachting blazer.

Increasingly, the other members of the Detours felt Dawson didn't fit in, and suddenly he found himself out of the band, to be replaced briefly by Gabby Connolly, vocalist with the Bel-Airs, another group on the same circuit as the Detours. But he too departed after the Detours appeared as support on the same bill to Johnny Kidd and the Pirates. Roger was mightily impressed at how the Pirates managed to produce a fully rounded sound with a line-up of just guitar, bass guitar and drums. This was partly due to the guitar work of the hugely gifted Mick Green. But the idea of just a trio of musicians behind a lead singer appealed to Roger, who finally abandoned the guitar to take on the job of lead singer full-time. The stripped-down line-up threw on Pete Townshend, in particular, and John Entwistle an extra burden of fleshing out the sound of the band behind Roger's vocals.

If the move to lead singer was partly Roger's way of asserting his authority over the other members of the Detours, particularly Pete, it inevitably caused new friction between him and Pete. By necessity, Pete's guitar now had to make a bigger impact and he was not backward in making his case about how and what the Detours should play. But, in Roger's mind, the Detours had always been his band. Now it was Roger up front, Roger taking centre stage. He physically positioned himself as the focal point of the Detours and was ever more determined to call the shots and dictate what material they played. 'When the band started I was a shit singer,' said Roger. 'They didn't need a singer in those days, they needed somebody who could fight and that was me.'

The antagonism between Townshend and Daltrey was evident from the very start. Pete, the creative art student, appeared to be looking sneeringly down his long nose at Roger, the factory labourer, and Roger didn't like that one little bit. Much of the hostility can be attributed to the varying attitudes towards the Detours. Roger was the one who lived the band and he felt that, given the chance, Pete would prefer to laze in bed all day smoking a joint.

Roger had a notoriously quick temper and he argued constantly with the guitarist. But while Pete would aggressively state his case with verbal dexterity, Roger preferred to use his fists to win the argument and demonstrate that he was the one running the show. 'He'd punctuate his decisions with punches,' was how John Entwistle described it. Doug Sandom was more direct: 'Roger and Pete were always at each other's throats. It was nothing to see Roger smack him in the nose at rehearsals.' Ironically, this bristling aggression, antagonism and bitterness was increasingly reflected in the group's musical output and approach on stage, giving them a unique edge and an exciting whiff of danger.

On the pop circuit the Detours liked to play very loudly and so were usually able to blow rival groups off the stage with their energetic and inventive cover versions of other people's hits. But Roger was keen that his band should not appear inferior just because they were only a trio of musicians, unlike the quartets playing four instruments who were springing up in the wake of the Beatles. The Detours were always loud, but one trick the band latched on to in order to gain superiority over their rivals was to at least appear to be pumping out more decibels than other groups. To that end, Roger began building ever-bigger cabinets for the group's speakers. 'We hit on the idea of having the biggest cabinets you've ever seen in your life, yet inside we'd have this little 12-inch speaker in the bottom. People used to come and see us and say: "They must be good, look at the size of their gear."'

The Detours' collective sound took on an altogether different dimension after the drummer's seat fell vacant. Doug Sandom, who was ten years older than the other band members, quit after an especially ugly row. He had never seen eye to eye with Pete, in particular, and now he had had enough of the sniping at his age. Though not entirely unexpected, Sandom's decision to quit nevertheless shocked Roger, but there was to be no backtracking on either side. Almost two years after he had joined the Detours, Sandom played his last gig on 13 April 1964 and Roger was forced to resort to finding session drummers to keep the band on the road.

Two weeks after Sandom's departure, the band were performing at one of their regular venues, the Oldfield Hotel in Greenford, when Roger was approached between their first and second set by a drunken lad from the audience who boasted that the pal he had brought along to see the Detours could play the drums a whole lot better than the man seated behind the drum kit that night. Since Roger figured that this was more than possible and bordered on highly likely, he invited the lad to come up on stage and prove it.

From out of the crush stepped a youth kitted out in brown shirt, brown tie, brown suit and brown shoes, all topped off with hair dyed a strange ginger colour. 'He looked just like a little ginger-bread man,' remembered Entwistle.

Gingerbread man settled himself behind the kit and Roger instantly put to him The Who's acid test for drummers. 'Can you play "Roadrunner"?' he asked, mindful that most stickmen he had encountered had fallen short when asked to lay down the beat for the Bo Diddley number. Gingerbread man not only played it faultlessly, ginger head bobbing up and down and swivelling from side to side, but he did it with such panache, force and wild abandon, sticks streaking through the air, that he broke the pedal of the bass drum which the session drummer had owned for 20 years, and managed to inflict grievous harm on the high hat into the bargain.

Roger was blown away by Keith Moon's distinctive drumming style and his sheer energy. It reminded him of a jet engine starting up. John and Pete also knew at once they had found their man. Before the evening was out, Keith Moon was in.

After the gig Gingerbread man was to be found enjoying a triumphant beer seated at the bar. His virtuoso display caused Roger to seek him out. Gingerbread man introduced himself as Keith Moon from Wembley, a plasterer and currently drummer with the Beachcombers, a surf band riding the wave of popularity generated by America's Beach Boys. What he didn't let on to Roger was that his outrageous ginger hair was the result of a dismal effort to dye his locks blond to look like a Californian beach boy. Strikingly different Moon's hair may have been, but it was his availability as a drummer that Roger was interested in. He asked Moon what he was doing the following Monday and, when he replied he was free, Roger told him there was a gig available. 'If you want to come, we'll pick you up in the van,' said Roger, leaving Moon dumbstruck.

'They said they'd come by at seven. And that was it,' Moon recalled many years later, still incredulous about the moment he found himself recruited as the last component of the group that would take the world of rock music by storm. 'Nobody ever said: "You're in." They just said: "What are you doing Monday?"'

He may have been bemused at how it all happened, but Moon recognised that joining the band was a step up for him. The Beachcombers were regularly playing on the same circuit as the Detours and Moon knew they had built up a good reputation. But while the Beachcombers went in for California-style girls-cars-and-surf harmony pop numbers like Jan and Dean's 'Bucket T' and the singalong 'Barbara Ann' by the Regents, the Detours socked it to their audiences large and loud. The two groups were very different, but Moon had got fed up with people coming up to him to say the Detours were much the better of the two.

While promoter Bob Druce sent the Detours out to various venues in and around London, it was locally, at the Goldhawk Social Club in Shepherd's Bush, that the band established a stronghold. They also built up a following in Hertfordshire thanks to appearances at the Trade Union Hall in Watford. But Roger's ambitions for the Detours received a setback when *Thank Your Lucky Stars*, a popular TV programme of the day which showcased the latest groups and sounds, introduced viewers to an Irish band called the Detours. Having tried so hard to build up a reputation for his own Detours, Roger was now faced with no other choice than to change the name of his band. Millions of viewers had seen the TV show and he didn't want any confusion with the Irish outfit it had featured.

He called the others together after a gig and told them they simply had to come up with a new name very quickly, something catchy and distinctive. That night Roger drove them all back to Pete's flat and they sat down with Pete's good friend Richard Barnes and chewed over possible new names. Among the suggestions were 'No One', 'the Group' and 'the Hair'. Then Barnes came up with 'The Who'. Eventually everyone dispersed for the night and next morning when Roger called round to pick up Pete to look at some new equipment, he told him: 'It's "The Who", innit?'

It was 'The Who' – but not all the time. Under the guidance of two new managers, Helmut Gorden, who handled the financial side of running the band, and an enterprising publicist by the name of Pete Meaden, they called themselves the High Numbers for a while. Meaden set about creating an image for the band as the first genuine Mod group, and in Meaden-speak 'the High Numbers' meant the tops. Conveniently, the word 'high' also evoked the amphetamines that the thrill-seeking Mods were taking to keep themselves awake.

The march of the Mods in England had already begun, a youth subculture soon to turn into a teenage stampede as a new generation of youngsters became obsessed with themselves, their clothes, their hair, their pep pills and their scooters, and fought running battles with Harley-riding rockers in leather biker jackets on southern beaches on Bank Holidays. Importantly, the Mods wanted new music to match their trendy new lives, and Meaden seized the moment to try to fulfil his dream of creating a group who were exactly the same on stage as their audience. While Beatles and Stones fans grew their hair long, Meaden packed Roger, Pete, Keith and John off to the barber to have their cut short. Roger's hair was naturally curly but he complied with Meaden's wishes and tried to brush it straight all the time.

Meaden also insisted the group dress in a new and hip way, kitting Roger out in an Ivy League seersucker suit or a cool white jacket, smart black trousers and snappy two-tone shoes. Roger balked at first at what he then regarded as prissy outfits. He was anxious not to look a prat or a pansy in front of his pals. He was very skinny, but he had a big chest and broad shoulders, which he felt were not naturally suited to Mod fashions. Even though he was less than comfortable in some of the outfits, he fell in line with Meaden's way of thinking. When the publicist succeeded in getting the band into a studio to record their first single for Fontana, Roger was photographed in the same white jacket, black trousers and eye-catching shoes for the promotional material.

'The first authentic Mod record', as it was billed, comprised two Meaden-manipulated numbers, 'I'm the Face' and 'Zoot Suit'. Meaden borrowed melody lines from the Showmen's 'Country Fool' and bluesman Slim Harpo's 'Got Love If You Want It' and imposed over them his own lyrics which reflected the Mod craze. 'I'm the Face' referred to the most self-assured, assertive dancers in Mod clubs and 'Zoot Suit' to a Mod's sartorial style. 'I'm the snappiest dresser right down to my inch-wide tie,' ran one of the lines Roger sang.

'Pete Meaden thought we could pick up on the Mod thing,' said Roger, 'and he was very right because Mods had no focal point at all, and The Who became that, even though we were really a little bit old to be a real part of it.'

The debut single by the High Numbers was released on 3 July 1964, but Fontana pressed just 1,000 copies and, even though

Meaden secured some media coverage, it failed to take off. Only around 500 copies were shifted, despite the efforts of John Entwistle's granny, who was said to have bought two dozen. It was a depressing result which left Roger downcast and desperately disappointed, especially when Fontana, who had recorded the group on a one-off basis, looked at the poor sales of 'I'm the Face/Zoot Suit' and decided not to take up an option to make another record with the High Numbers.

CHAPTER THREE

THE BIRTH OF THE WHO

How were these four bug-uglies, with their demented drummer thrashing around in the background, so able to convince me that this was as exciting an event as Wagner? There was a Satanic quality about them, and I knew at once this was the group I'd been looking for.

Kit Lambert on seeing the High Numbers
for the first time

One sunlit Tuesday evening in July 1964, the burly bouncers on duty at the Railway Tavern, a pub-cum-club close to Harrow and Wealdstone Tube station in north-west London, watched dubiously as a dapper young man they had not seen before pulled up outside in his Volkswagen Beetle. His name was Kit Lambert and he was on a mission. As he opened his car door he could just about make out an insistent muffled throb which told him that the beat group he had specifically come to see and hear were indeed performing inside.

To the practised eye of the bouncers, Lambert's custom-made grey suit was far too smart and expensive to figure in the wardrobe of the average Mod who frequented the Railway Tavern to see the latest pop groups. Not only that but the scooter was then the favoured mode of transport for Mods, and Lambert's Beetle looked out of place parked among the rows of Lambrettas lined up outside the pub. The bouncers' suspicions were raised immediately. In a venue with an official capacity of

180, they were aware that at least three times that number of fans were already packed inside to hear a promising new band who had been given a regular Tuesday-evening gig by local public demand.

As the stranger strolled towards the entrance, the bouncers eyed him nervously, wondering if he was an official from the local authority checking out the venue's compliance with noise and safety regulations. Or, they figured, he could even be a representative of the brewery who owned the pub, surreptitiously making a spot check on the way the place was being run. But, as he approached the door, he eased their fears by first asking them the name of the band performing that night and then explaining he was there as a film producer looking for a prospective pop group that he could build a project around.

Admission granted, Kit Lambert was greeted by a sight and sound that would remain indelibly etched in his memory for the rest of his life. He found the heat unbearably oppressive and stifling, since it was the practice of the promoter to keep the radiators turned up to the very limit, even in summer, to help create a steamy club atmosphere. The windows had also been deliberately blacked out to keep the venue dark and, to inject something of a sinful, edgy ambience into what was really only a pub function room, the owner had also removed all the lightbulbs bar two, which he had painted pink.

It took Kit a few seconds to adjust his eyes to the dim, smoky light and his ears to the deafening music pounding from the speakers parked on a primitive stage made out of beer crates and table tops. Scanning the room, he saw a crush of several hundred Mods thronging excitedly around a band who were pumping out the loudest rock music he'd ever heard. What struck Kit particularly was the way the predominantly male audience, standing shoulder to shoulder, appeared to be some form of excited extension of the musical dynamics they were witnessing from the band. Within minutes he felt himself drawn into the commotion and excitement generated by the sheer energy with which the High Numbers belted out their high-decibel music.

'The atmosphere in there was fantastic, the room was black and hot. Steaming hot. And the audience seemed hypnotised by the wild music, with the feedback that Pete Townshend was already producing from his guitar and amplifier,' Lambert told the authors.

On first impression, they were hardly the best-looking quartet he had seen. 'The lead singer wasn't very tall and a bit spotty, the guitarist's face was dominated by his nose, the bass guitarist's looks were unremarkable and the drummer, mouth agape, just looked wild. But they absolutely fascinated me,' recalled Lambert.

The man who was to play a crucial role in piloting Roger Daltrey and his band to stardom summed up his reaction to that July night thus: 'How were these four bug-uglies, with their demented drummer thrashing around in the background, so able to convince me that this was as exciting an event as Wagner? There was a Satanic quality about them. and I knew at once this was the group I'd been looking for.'

Born Christopher Sebastian Lambert, the son of Constant Lambert, an illustrious English composer most notably acclaimed for his ballet music, Kit came from a talented and artistic family which also included the landscape painter George Washington Lambert. Kit himself was a product of Lancing College, a highly regarded English public school, where his adolescent dreams and ambitions were as lofty as the school's magnificent chapel perched high on a hill near the Sussex coast. Even in his early teens, Kit displayed the flamboyant nature which was to colour his all too brief life: he died in April 1981 after falling down the stairs at his mother's home in Fulham, west London. His outlook set him apart from other pupils. He was always telling anyone who would listen that he was going to set the arts world alight in one way or another.

From Lancing, Lambert went on to Trinity College, Oxford, where his interest in movies led to his becoming a notable treasurer of the university's Film Society. 'I was the first person to put it back into the black,' he said. 'I did it by running advertisements between the reels of the films, and by running films four nights a week instead of one.' He further pursued his love of films by later studying at the film school of the University of Paris, where he eked out his £40-a-month grant by living in a garret on a diet of potatoes and very little else.

Lambert's sense of adventure next took him to Brazil after he volunteered to be a cameraman on an expedition which aimed to chart the world's longest undescended river, the Iriri. Chillingly, the expedition ended in the horrific death of a close friend, killed by a cannibalistic tribe.

Back in England, Kit had various jobs in the film industry before becoming a director's assistant on major movies such as the James Bond film *From Russia with Love* and the action-packed war epic *The Guns of Navarone.* He recalled: 'My last and most successful job in films was when I was on the Disney movie *The Moonspinners*, which was notable for the fact that it starred the former child actress Hayley Mills getting her first screen kiss. Disney gave it the whole big treatment and the unit I was looking after eventually amounted to 375 people, five different camera crews working simultaneously. Walt Disney came over in person with his wife to see the shooting and was impressed enough by what I was doing to double my salary.

'When I got back to London, the Beatles had just done the Royal Command Performance and rock 'n' roll had taken London by siege. It had come to my notice and to the notice of another assistant director, Chris Stamp, brother of actor Terry, that we were working on movies which cost £1 million to make, while other people were cheaply making really bad rock 'n' roll films which were jumping ahead in the queue. They were made on small budgets and doing really well, even though they were crap. So I was determined that, with my savings and bonus from *The Moonspinners*, I'd make a much better pop film than any that was around.

'Led by the Beatles, there had been an explosion of beat groups and, in partnership with Chris Stamp, we started searching after work each night for groups we could set a film around. It had all started in Liverpool with the Beatles, Gerry and the Pacemakers, and the Searchers, then in Manchester with the Hollies and Herman's Hermits, and even Newcastle had come up with a group, the Animals. So we felt London simply had to come up with one too.'

Together, Lambert and Stamp were an unlikely yet formidable combination. Lambert was born in Knightsbridge and spoke in upper-class rounded vowels. Stamp was working-class, from Plaistow, in London's East End. But both were ambitious and Lambert's colourful drive was complemented by Stamp's street savvy, gained from his youth as the son of a Thames tugboatman. They operated from 113 Ivor Court, a rented one-bedroom flat on the ninth floor of a block of apartments in Gloucester Place, off Baker Street. It was hardly luxury living: 'There I was, on a narrow bed with cardboard on the floor, Chris Stamp sleeping on the sofa and Mike Shaw, an associate, having to sleep bolt upright in a chair,' Kit reminisced.

From this base the three set off separately of an evening to scour the pubs and clubs for pop groups in areas of London they had divided up between them. They checked out gigs advertised in local papers and made notes of other dates on posters and hoardings. It was a frustrating process. Many a night proved fruitless. Each of the trio knew they were looking for a group who stood out from all the others, and each would often ascertain within minutes whether a band was suitable or not. Other groups required further hours of monitoring and debate before being ultimately rejected.

After a few months of unsuccessful trawling, Lambert and Stamp's funds were running low. They were reluctant to dip into the money set aside to make their film, so Stamp went off to work as assistant director on John Ford's movie *Young Cassidy*, which was being shot in Ireland. It was while Stamp was there that Lambert came upon the High Numbers at the Railway Tavern in suburban north-west London. That night he drove home convinced he had found exactly what he was looking for.

Kit was excited enough about the band to contact Stamp in Dublin immediately and urge him to come back to England on his weekend off from filming to see the High Numbers for himself. His enthusiasm was persuasive, and Stamp flew back to check out the band at Watford's Trade Union Hall on Saturday, 18 July 1964. His journey was delayed, so he was able to catch only the last 15 minutes of the High Numbers' set, but it was enough for him to agree that Lambert's assessment of the band was spot on. 'I was knocked out,' he later told the *Observer*. 'But the excitement I felt wasn't coming from the group. I couldn't get near enough. It was coming from the people blocking my way.'

Wasting no time, Lambert hired a gym the following day at Holland Park Comprehensive School in Campden Hill Road, west London, for an informal audition and the group were signed to feature in a 20-minute documentary depicting their rise from obscurity to fame. He recalled: 'We made a film within days of meeting them, but the money ran out while we were making it. Then it occurred to me overnight that we should manage them. I was totally ignorant of management and hadn't done anything like it before so I knew it would be a gamble. I didn't know anything about the music business, either, so that was a gamble too, especially because the better sort of R&B music that they were starting to play hadn't made the charts then. The charts were dominated by people like Cliff Richard and Adam Faith.'

Lambert did, however, know enough about the entertainment industry and important figures within it to help him engineer a buyout of the group's contract from their existing management. Pete Meaden and Helmut Gorden were ousted. But, despite the time and money the Lambert-Stamp partnership had spent on the movie of the High Numbers, and despite the pair's flashy appearance, Roger, in particular, was far from convinced they were the right men to put in place the springboard to success that he craved for his group.

With his upper-class accent, Lambert at first reminded Roger of the plummy tones he had encountered from the more well-to-do pupils he despised at his old school. A visit to the duo's 'office', which didn't exactly smack of entrepreneurial style and efficiency, made Roger and the others understandably wary about committing themselves to them.

But their minds were made up when Lambert, to blow away their doubts, flamboyantly took the four of them to one of the smartest eating places in town, an expensive Chinese restaurant in the Edgware Road, patronised by many of the top stars of the day. Lambert was out to impress but, unfortunately for him, the only star they spotted was fading singer Dorothy Squires. 'Happily, thank God, she wasn't singing at the piano,' Lambert recalled. 'Anyway, I'd whisked The Who from the gutter to the smartest restaurant in London and sat them down and they said: "Kit, we love you to death, but you're a jerk. You haven't got any contacts or an office, and you haven't got a coat with a fur collar. And you wouldn't be able to get us a record deal and get it into the Top 20."

'So then I said: "Listen, you c***s, what do you mean I can't get you into the Top 20? I'll bet you your wages and more I can." I actually threw down the gauntlet on a Chinese table cloth. I remember Roger Daltrey's face turned into a mask of clay when I suggested a week and a half's wages should be the stake. His face completely blanched.

'Ten nights' wages I was betting them, as they were going out then at £12 a night and there were four of them. It was my £120 against each of their four £30s. Pete Townshend, another Taurus like me and born on the same day, was too superstitious to touch it with a bargepole. But Roger punted in, and so did Keith. Then

Entwistle, the mean one, the meanest of the mean, said: "I'll come in for a tenner."

'I'd challenged all the four boys one by one to a bet and followed up by offering them a minimum guarantee of £20 a week. I guaranteed this weird collection of people £1,000 a year each to give up their jobs in their garages, their sheet-metal factories, their tax offices, their art schools. "You're great," I said. "So fuck off – you're either in or out. I'll guarantee you your £1,000 a year with my money and money from the sale of my father's portrait which now hangs in the National Portrait Gallery." In fact, I sold everything I had, never mind the 15 years of scrimping and saving that had gone on.'

Once Roger, Pete, John and Keith had all agreed they would allow Lambert and Stamp to take over their management, there was a formal contract to be drawn up and signed. This was not as simple an undertaking as it might have been since each member of the High Numbers was under 21 and would therefore, by law, need the consent of their parents. John Entwistle's parents were all for it, and Keith Moon's and Pete Townshend's were swayed by Lambert's confident assertion that he would make them famous and rich. Pete's parents recognised that Lambert was from a musical family, just like their own son. But Harry and Irene Daltrey were not so sure about Kit Lambert.

Kit paid a visit to their home one Sunday afternoon to meet them for the first time and to persuade them that Roger and his band had a great future. He exuded the confident air of a man who believed he really could take the High Numbers to fame and fortune and Harry was eventually won over by his enthusiastic demeanour. But Irene was still far from convinced. Although she fully understood and appreciated Roger was passionate about his music, she fretted that a career in pop music seemed to her quite literally a hit-or-miss life. Also, by then Roger was only nine months away from completing his apprenticeship at the sheet-metal factory and Irene understandably felt he should see out those few months and gain his union card before going fully professional as a singer.

Over cups of tea, Irene voiced her fears in front of Kit and Roger. Finally Roger began to win his mum over by assuring her that all her worries would disappear and she would be proud and pleased as punch once she started seeing him making appearances on the telly. In the end a compromise was reached by which Roger would keep paying his union dues so that he had a fully paid-up membership card and something to fall back on if his singing career didn't work out.

Although it was not written into Roger's contract, there was one other extremely important matter which Lambert wanted settled pretty swiftly. He firmly suggested it would be better if Roger would leave his teenage wife, Jackie, whom he had married after she fell pregnant. Although he stopped short of insisting on it, Lambert pointed out to Roger that he might have to take tough decisions and there could be painful casualties if he was going to dedicate himself to the band. This included his marriage.

In his early teens Roger had discovered what countless pop musicians before and since have learned to their pleasure – that playing a guitar is a magnet for girls, a passport to sex. On stage he was the focus of attention and with his tough-guy bravado he'd had no difficulty in attracting the prettiest girls who came to see the Detours, the High Numbers and The Who, as they in turn became. 'The fact is, as soon as you picked up a guitar, there was always a bird sitting on one end of it,' he would say gleefully. 'I wanted women and money, and rock 'n' roll gave me both.'

Even before he had reached the age of 18, Roger had been engaged twice. Both fiancées were local girls, both happened to be called Barbara, but neither managed to lead him up the aisle. Roger realised he was having too much fun and there were too many fish in the sea only too willing to be caught by a thrusting young would-be rock star. 'There'd always be girls hanging around him,' his sister Gillian once remembered. 'Roger was girl-mad. I don't know what they saw in him then because he was always so dominant and aggressive.'

While the two Barbaras nursed their broken hearts and watched their ex-fiancé take his steady steps up the pop ladder, it wasn't long before Roger found himself suddenly shedding his single status. He was just four weeks out of his teens when he married pretty Jacqueline Rickman at Wandsworth Register Office in south-west London, on 28 March 1964. His bride, whom he'd met at a gig in Putney, was just 16.

Fittingly, top of the charts in the week that Roger dutifully put his bachelor days behind him was a record called 'Little Children' by Billy J. Kramer and the Dakotas. Not only were Roger and Jacqueline little more than children themselves and terribly young to get married, but Jackie was also by now carrying Roger's child. 'It was one of those where pregnancy comes first, then marriage,' said Roger. Less than five months later their son, Simon, was born at The Downs in Wimbledon.

For his wedding, Roger chose as his best man John Reader, a merchant seaman friend who was a sometime drummer with the Detours and was also occasionally roped in to act as the band's roadie. After the brief ceremony the young pregnant Easter bride and her embryo rock star husband repaired to Jacqueline's family home in Putney to celebrate with close family and friends, including members of the British beat group Johnny Kidd and the Pirates, best known for their 1960 chart-topper 'Shakin' All Over'. Roger had become friends with them all because his band had often been the opening support act at their gigs. Much later, 'Shakin' All Over' would become part of The Who's onstage repertoire and feature on their classic album *Live at Leeds*.

The following morning, Easter Sunday, Roger awoke on his first day as a married man to the dramatic and exciting news for pop-starved British teenagers that a 'pirate' radio ship had started broadcasting pop music on British airwaves from three and a half miles off the Essex coast. A young disc jockey called Simon Dee had that morning made an historic announcement from a 763-ton vessel anchored in the North Sea: 'Good morning, ladies and gentlemen,' said Dee. 'This is Radio Caroline, broadcasting on 199, your all-day music station.' Before the day was over, a sizeable audience had built up, almost entirely by word of mouth. Like millions of others of his age, Roger sat up and listened.

Radio Caroline's broader musical message was that that there was a whole new generation of pop fans in Britain that the BBC's radio programmes were failing to cater for. By broadcasting offshore and out of reach of British law, Radio Caroline and the other pop pirate ships which followed in its wake, were able to offer the Beatles generation a non-stop diet of the latest hits. For up-and-coming groups like The Who, the pirates were to be a godsend. Less than a year later Radio Caroline was to play a crucial part in 'breaking' The Who by giving their first record, 'I Can't Explain', regular airplay.

Radio Caroline claimed seven million listeners only three weeks after it had gone on the air for the first time. Eventually the pirates would claim a total audience of 25 million before the Government introduced a bill to scuttle the radio ships, which in turn led to the launch of the BBC's own station devoted to pop music, Radio 1.

That Sunday, 29 March 1964, as Roger and Jacqueline began their life together as man and wife, all the teenage talk was of the birth of Radio Caroline. And Jacqueline was left in no doubt as to the kind of married life she could expect to lead with Roger. Day one for Jackie, the new Mrs Daltrey, began with her husband travelling down to the Sussex coast to play a gig at the Florida Rooms adjoining Brighton Aquarium.

Although well intentioned and anxious to do the decent thing, Roger found it hard to make a go of the marriage. He was still very young, with a head full of dreams for the Detours, and after working all day at the sheet-metal factory to ensure he had a regular weekly wage, he would try to skive off early most nights to go gigging with the band. It was hardly conducive to a settled married life and impending fatherhood. Often it would be the small hours before he returned to Jacqueline after a gig, if at all. Some nights after playing it was easier and less tiring to sleep in the group's van at the side of the road than to drive for hours to get back to the one-room council flat he and Jacqueline were renting in Wandsworth.

Irene Daltrey was dubious about the marriage almost from the start. She couldn't see how Jacqueline, pretty, quiet and kind though she was, could fit into the rock 'n' roll world to which her son was so committed. 'She was like the girl next door and just out of place in all that scene,' Irene once confided. 'It couldn't last.'

She was right: it didn't last. 'I stuck it for a few months before I went back to living in a furniture van which The Who were using as transport,' Roger recalled. 'I knew that if I didn't move away from her in those early days, I would be a sheet-metal worker for life.'

Given their tender years and their difficult circumstances, it's debatable whether Roger and Jackie's marriage was ever going to survive. But there's no doubt that Lambert actively encouraged Roger to put the band before Jackie and make The Who his whole life. A close former associate of Lambert says: 'Being homosexual, Kit perhaps didn't attach as much importance to the institution of marriage as he might have done. He recognised Roger had done the decent thing in getting married and respected him for that. But he felt family responsibilities would hold Roger, and therefore the band, back. He had grand plans for the group and questioned whether Roger's commitment to the band would wane under the weight of trying also to be a proper husband and father.'

The pull of The Who was too strong for Roger. His desire to make a name and a career for himself in rock music was all he had thought about and strived for since he had first become hooked by the music of Presley and Lonnie Donegan. 'It was a choice between staying married or the group. I chose the group,' he says simply.

Lambert was especially anxious that Roger should appear to be a single man so that he would seem 'available' in the eyes of the posse of young girls who were now following the group in ever-larger numbers. It also wouldn't do, argued Lambert, for the lead singer of such an abrasive band with such a strong male following to be seen as a cosy family man with a wife and young kid at home.

As a natural consequence of being on the road, Roger gradually spent less and less time at home. Eventually he moved out of the modest marital home and took up uncomfortable, semi-permanent residence in The Who's equipment van. This unsettling state of affairs continued for around six months, but Roger somehow managed to stay cheerful about his circumstances. He consoled himself he was really no different from the long-distance lorry driver who would settle down at night for a kip in the cab. There was also an undeniably attractive feeling of freedom, he decided, in being able to park the van anywhere he chose, relying on visits to pals for a wash and brush-up and maybe breakfast too if he was lucky.

Despite this nomadic lifestyle, Roger didn't shirk his family duties and every week sent money from his earnings back to the wife from whom he had separated so soon after their wedding.

In January 1968 Jacqueline applied for a divorce. So successful was Lambert in covering up Roger's marital status that many Who fans had no idea he had been married, and had a son to boot, until news of the divorce became public.

Although it would be May 1970 before the divorce was granted, Roger took full advantage of being footloose and fancy-free once more following his separation from Jackie. He was soon back playing the field. And for the lead singer of a pop band on the up, there was no shortage of girls to choose from. In Sweden, when The Who were touring Scandinavia, Roger had a brief affair which produced a son, Mateus, whose existence was not made public until Roger chose to talk openly for the first time about him in 1980.

CHAPTER FOUR

I CAN'T EXPLAIN

*The High Numbers was a nothing name. It implied the
Top 20, but The Who seemed perfect for them. It was
impersonal. It couldn't be dated.*

Chris Stamp

While Kit Lambert and Chris Stamp were able to witness for
themselves the growing impact Roger and his band nightly were
having on the audiences who came to see them, the duo were desperate to land the High Numbers a recording contract. It was the
natural progression for any aspiring pop group and the co-managers urgently needed to generate more money from the band if
they were to keep the group going.

The pair had come fresh to the music business. In other words,
they knew very little about it, apart from the fact that it seemed to
them that, if you got it right, untold riches appeared to be forth-
coming. Thanks to Beatlemania, the music industry was
expanding fast, the Swinging Sixties were in full swing and London
was the coolest capital in the world. Music, art, photography, fashion, design were open to anyone with ideas, and Kit and Chris
were full of them. But a recording contract was not easy to come

by, especially as the band had already registered one failure with Fontana.

However, with the help of his friend Russ Conway, a popular light pianist who had enjoyed several bouncy instrumental hits for EMI, Lambert arranged an audition for the High Numbers in Studio 3 at EMI's recording studios at 3 Abbey Road, St John's Wood, the studios later made world-famous by the Beatles.

EMI A&R man John Burgess was persuaded by Conway to have a listen to a few numbers as a favour. Obligingly, Conway even went so far as to lend Lambert and the band his Rolls-Royce so that Roger, Pete, John and Keith could arrive for the audition at least looking like they were hitting the big time even if this was hardly the style to which they were accustomed. Normally they all squashed uncomfortably into Lambert's Beetle.

Lambert came away from the audition fearing the worst, although there had been some positive reaction to Roger's vocals. 'They thought Roger had a nice cutting voice,' he remembered of the try-out, 'but they felt the band were not harmonious enough for EMI. They felt the backing voices were like a singing crow compared with the Beatles. It also became clear that the band had to start writing their own material like the Beatles.' Lambert urged Pete Townshend, especially, to take note.

The formal rejection from EMI came in a letter written to Lambert on 22 October 1964, in which Burgess explained that he had listened again and again to the results of the test session but still could not decide whether or not the High Numbers had anything to offer. He had the good grace, however, to wish them all the luck in the world if in the meantime they had signed up with another record company – which they had not.

Undaunted, Lambert persisted in doing the rounds of record companies and producers. He and Stamp also took the decision to change the band's name once again. They would revert to 'The Who'. Lambert, especially, liked the name as it had attractive marketing possibilities and scope for various judicious puns. The High

Numbers, he finally decided, sounded more like something out of a bingo game. Stamp agreed: 'The High Numbers was a nothing name,' he said. 'It implied the Top 20, but The Who seemed perfect for them. It was impersonal. It couldn't be dated.' Lambert concurred, saying: 'The Who was a gimmick name. Journalists could write "The Why of The Who" and people had to go through a boring ritual of question and answer: "Have you heard The Who?" "the who?" "The Who." It was an invitation to corniness and we were in a corny world.'

Eventually Lambert turned to Shel Talmy, an independent producer who was making a name for himself masterminding hits for another British group, the Kinks. Chicago-born Talmy had started out as a recording engineer for a small company in Los Angeles before heading for Europe for a month to see the sights and suss out the pop scene in England. While in London, he contacted Decca and, having nothing to lose, with great panache and self-aggrandisement he cheekily overstated to the label's bosses his achievements and credentials as a record producer in LA and was given work on the spot.

Entrusted by Decca with a promising Irish trio called the Bachelors, Talmy first rehearsed them hard for a couple of months and taught them how to harmonise, then took them into a studio to produce a single called 'Charmaine', which took all of 15 minutes to complete. Decca loved it, especially when the record went to number six in the charts early in January 1963.

Talmy's reputation soared and he secured himself a unique position as an independent producer who worked for Decca but was also able to find other artists to record for other labels. Having grown up with rock 'n' roll, Talmy was constantly searching for a decent rock group in England to record and the Kinks virtually fell into his lap when he bumped into their manager at Mills Music in Denmark Street, home to many of London's top music publishers. A demo disc by the Kinks was being hawked around, and Talmy agreed to give it a listen and was instantly impressed. 'I thought they were really sensational,' he said, and swiftly arranged to record them for Pye. In September 1964 'You Really Got Me', produced by Talmy, took the Kinks to the top of the charts, and the Talmy-produced follow-up, 'All Day and All of the Night', was another smash hit, reaching number two.

Talmy's success didn't go unnoticed by Kit Lambert. Happily for Kit, he knew a girl who worked for Talmy and via her he invited Talmy to hear The Who in action at a church hall he hired specially for the occasion. Talmy liked what he heard and the way the group looked. He was convinced they were a hit band and was confident enough in his judgement to spend his own money to prove it. Early in November 1964 he booked The Who into the London studios of Pye Records in Great Cumberland Place, near Marble Arch. There he produced 'I Can't Explain', a Pete Townshend composition with guitar riffs which owed not a little to the staccato chords of the Kinks' smash hit 'You Really Got Me'. Modelling The Who's first record on a proven formula made sense and seemed to Talmy to be the safest bet. Just three months earlier The Who had been on the same bill as the Kinks at the Opera House in Blackpool, and Townshend's blatant derivation for 'I Can't Explain' may well have been influenced by watching the Kinks on stage.

Studio time costs money, and since it was his own money that Talmy was using to fund the recording session, he liked to take a thoroughly professional approach to the business of recording. No drinking, no eating, was the order of the day, and to get the job done as efficiently and as quickly as possible Talmy hired a session drummer and a highly talented young session guitarist by the name of Jimmy Page to help out. Talmy also brought in harmony trio the Ivy League because, as he later bluntly put it: 'The Who's backing vocals sucked.' Roger was shocked when he arrived to find Talmy had lined up these auxiliaries. If Lambert and Stamp knew that this would be the case, they had not let on to Roger.

Pete Townshend was not unduly alarmed to discover Jimmy

Page was to feature strongly in the recording session. Pete was by now acquainted with Jimmy, later to become the grandiloquent guitar-playing icon of the archetypal rock quartet of the seventies, Led Zeppelin. Jimmy assured Pete he was simply there to give some weight to the guitar and double the rhythm guitar on the overdubs. But Keith Moon was furious to find another drummer assembling his kit in the studio. He was having none of it and vented his fury with a volley of foul-mouthed abuse before tossing the rival drummer's kit out of the studio. 'Get out or I'll fucking kill you,' was Keith's parting shot.

Once the fracas had subsided, the session progressed smoothly enough. Roger and the band were in the studio for just a couple of hours, and the finished record emerged at just over two minutes long. As well as taking the lead vocals, Roger played percussion on 'I Can't Explain', and he also played harmonica on the B side, a Talmy composition called 'Bald Headed Woman'.

Looking back, Roger has frequently expressed his satisfaction at the way 'I Can't Explain' turned out. He was proud of it because it was an original song by Pete Townshend and he felt it encapsulated the energy and testosterone of The Who at that time. But, at that point, Roger was not altogether comfortable at having to switch from the blues vocals he favoured to the more commercial pop style of 'I Can't Explain'.

It was nevertheless a bold and explosive debut for The Who, a song about the frustrations of being unable to express oneself, not just to the girl you were dating but to the world in general. The lyrics of 'I Can't Explain' played on emotional inarticulacy and struck such a chord with teenagers that shortly after the record's release Townshend was allegedly approached by a gang of kids in Shepherd's Bush begging him to write more songs in a similar vein. And it is testament to the strength of the song that 'I Can't Explain' would, for many years to come, nearly always be the number The Who used to open their live shows.

With the release of 'I Can't Explain' still some eight weeks away,

Lambert and Stamp redoubled their efforts to get The Who known in areas other than their established strongholds of Shepherd's Bush and Hertfordshire. An opportunity soon presented itself which was to prove crucial to the group's breakthrough – the chance of a residency at the Marquee club, right in the heart of central London's entertainment scene.

The Marquee had originally thrived in Oxford Street, drawing fans of traditional jazz. But now it had moved to 90 Wardour Street in Soho, reinventing itself as the place to go for hard R&B after London's hippest musical community began leaning more towards this kind of music, played first by American blues artists and then by the likes of Alexis Korner and Long John Baldry, seminal British figures on the London R&B scene in the mid-sixties.

In the face of the beat group explosion triggered by the Beatles in Liverpool and the mushrooming R&B scene in London, trad jazz was proving increasingly unappetising musical fare at the Marquee – especially on Tuesday nights, normally the slowest night of the week. In a bold move, Lambert and Stamp approached promoter Ziggy Jackson with a proposal that The Who should take over the club each Tuesday. The deal guaranteed Jackson a fee but a profit for The Who only if they pulled in big crowds.

'They were just about to close the Marquee down on Tuesday nights, so it was worth the gamble,' Lambert recalled. 'But there was no one in the West End of London on Tuesday nights, as I discovered later when trying to pack the place with an audience for The Who. Very few people were out – everyone was broke by Tuesday.'

The turnout was around 30 for The Who's first Tuesday appearance, on the rainy night of 24 November 1964, which was not only disappointing for Roger and everyone connected with The Who but represented a considerable hole in Lambert and Stamp's finances. Ziggy Jackson and the band still had to be paid. The following week it was time for Lambert to call in the cavalry in the shape of the Hundred Faces, an exclusive club he and Stamp had dreamed up which consisted of hard-core fans of The Who picked out largely by Lambert himself. 'I'd go to places and anyone who was an outstandingly good dancer I'd make a member of the Hundred Faces club,' he explained. 'That was a club we created which gave members life free admission to Who concerts and a membership card they could show that they were one of the Hundred Faces in London.'

To swell the audience, Lambert arranged for a number of concessionary tickets to be printed which allowed entry for just two shillings and sixpence (25p) rather than the normal entry fee of five shillings. He and Stamp also paid £300 to have 1,500 arty fly-posters produced which advertised The Who's Tuesday-night residency with a distinctive arrow pointing upwards from the letter O (the biological symbol for male) and a picture of Pete Townshend, right arm raised at the top of his by now trademark windmill arc, ready to crash down on to the strings of his Rickenbacker guitar. In addition, Lambert came up with the slogan 'Maximum R&B', to be printed on both posters and tickets.

'So I had my private army of Mod fans of The Who, my Hundred Faces,' he recalled, 'and the next Tuesday night I'm going around with concession tickets beautifully printed out and Stamp and everyone from the office and other friends are handing them out to people around Marble Arch and Piccadilly Circus.'

The second Marquee gig, on 1 December 1964, pulled in an audience of 298, a considerable improvement, but 123 of those paid the cut-price two shillings and sixpence for their entrance ticket. After all the expenses and various percentage cuts had been taken into consideration, the total income was £18 18s and 2d. From this the band had to be paid, and Roger's earnings for the night amounted to a princely £2.

Lambert's persistence, however, gradually began to pay off. The Marquee, right in the heart of Soho, was not best placed for young west London Mods to get to after work or college. But Roger and the rest of the band, and not least Kit Lambert, were relieved to find around a hundred of them made it to the Marquee on the second Tuesday and within a month the audience had swelled to over 1,000, in the process beating the club's record, held until then by Manfred Mann. 'It happened so fast, it was amazing,' said Roger. 'You had the feeling anything could happen. We were the kids' group.'

It was all very well being known in Shepherd's Bush and Hertfordshire, but the Marquee residency was indeed priceless. Now, from the very centre of London, the word about The Who began to filter outwards, first to the Home Counties and in time far beyond.

'Maximum R&B' was not, in fact, a strict summary of The Who's set at the Marquee. A typical set included Bo Diddley's 'I'm a Man', Howlin' Wolf's 'Smokestack Lightning', Derek Martin's 'Daddy Rolling Stone', Rufus Thomas's 'Jump Back' and Chris Kenner's 'Land of 1000 Dances', but there would be a nod to jazz with Mose Allison's 'Young Man', a smattering of Motown with 'Dancing in the Street', 'Heatwave' and Marvin Gaye's 'Baby Don't You Do It', as well as James Brown's 'Please Please Please' and 'I Don't Mind'. Roger commented: 'I think that was the most interesting period in our career, because we made all those songs our own as just a three-instrument and vocal band.' Performing established Chicago blues numbers which could sound so similar night after night required improvisation to avoid monotony and spurred in particular Pete and John to experiment with ways to freshen up a song, expand the sound and give it a new but still authentic blues feel.

Perversely, The Who lost some of their following when they first concentrated on R&B, but Roger noted that once the band had enjoyed some success on record, their lost followers quickly returned. Later, when The Who were able to perform their own material, they left R&B to other groups that they had been vying with in this area, like the Yardbirds, the Pretty Things and the Downliners Sect.

With 'I Can't Explain' ready for release and audiences now heaving at the Marquee, it was looking good for The Who. And Lambert continued to stoke the fire. 'In those days pills – Blues as they were called – were part of the rock 'n' roll scene and at one club you even had a man with tickets on the left of the door and another man with the packet of Blues on the right. You paid ten shillings to get in and ten shillings for your Blues, including a performance by The Who of course. They particularly affected John Entwistle, who was able to sing an octave higher on these Blues, and at the Noreik in north London [a club in Tottenham] they were able to get those dazzling harmonies that could never be recaptured anywhere else.

'Actually, I was very strict in my attitude about drugs. I caught The Who on their very first concert when they were playing bottom of the bill to the Beatles and gave them a terrific roasting for smoking joints before they went on stage and was generally frightfully stern about these things. But now I found I was giving them Blues to make them sing better.

'I wanted to give Blues to my tame army of Mods, too, but I could hardly be seen as a promoter of a concert at the Marquee surreptitiously handing out Blues. So I discovered a wonderful substitute, a whisky and ginger ale, and all these Mods would be coming up to me saying: "Well, thanks, Kit. I'm getting almost as high on this as I did on the Blues. In fact, it's even better." There are probably 100 confirmed drunkards in Shepherd's Bush as a result of my tactics to try and create a warm and exciting atmosphere. But the whole idea was to build it up and make a Who gig at the Marquee sensational in itself. Soon we had queues right around the block.'

Ziggy Jackson was surprised but naturally delighted that Tuesday nights at the Marquee had proved such a success, and he promptly booked The Who for a run of 16 weeks, which he extended by another seven weeks when the band broke the club's audience record.

Despite full houses, Lambert reckoned that any profits he made were minimal. He found he was shelling out money on the group all too readily, especially on new equipment, for by now Pete Townshend had developed a penchant for harpooning his guitar through the stack of Marshall amps. At a time when the average working wage was £20 a week, Pete was most nights demolishing a £150 guitar bought on hire purchase.

Lambert was also having to cope with bitter rivalries between Roger and Pete, who was rapidly asserting increasing authority over The Who. 'Basically the Marquee deal was a rotten one for us financially,' said Lambert, 'and yet Pete Townshend was insisting on having new clothes to appear every week in front of his audience. Pete began refusing to appear unless we gave him new clothes every week.

'I got my revenge because I decided it was high time the band had some new material and so I'd get up at the crack of dawn and go around the exotic record shops in London that had American imports to try and find new songs. I'd find five new songs and tell Pete: "You won't get any new clothes unless you learn at least three of these songs before tonight." Roger and Pete always used to look down their noses at them because they thought I was stupid musically. But I told them: "If you don't, I'm going to go down the queue waiting to see The Who and tell everyone they're going to hear the same old crap as they heard last week. And I meant it." Then they'd come on stage with three new songs – and, of course, there would be a new jacket for Pete.'

It's not often that The Who are mentioned in the same breath as Sir Winston Churchill. But, bizarre and unlikely as it may seem, the band's first breakthrough on record owed more than a little to the passing of Sir Winston, Britain's wartime Prime Minister, illustrious statesman and the man recently voted overwhelmingly by millions of Britons as the Greatest Englishman.

'I Can't Explain' was released on 15 January 1965, which happened to be the day on which Sir Winston fell gravely ill after suffering a stroke. He was to die peacefully at the age of 90 nine days later, and his death was to provide Kit Lambert with an extraordinary slice of luck which he was quick to turn to full advantage.

As record launches go, 'I Can't Explain' could hardly have been more inauspicious. Roger and the rest of the band were desperately disappointed to find that only around 1,000 copies of the single had been pressed by Brunswick, the American arm of Decca. The record slipped out virtually unnoticed among a batch of other 45rpm Decca releases and Kit Lambert was especially annoyed that such apathy by the record company towards The Who's first release was mirrored by its minimalist promotional plans for the single.

Tony Hall, Decca's promotions manager at the time, told *Record World*: 'It was just another of some 20 releases that particular week. I remember Kit's frustrations vividly. I think he came into my office and made me promise to really "live" with the record over the weekend and to give him an honest opinion on the Monday. This I did, and I came in on the Monday morning convinced that with sufficient exposure this was a smash hit.'

By 14 February 1965, a month after its release, 'I Can't Explain' had sold enough copies to creep into the Top 50 at number 47. Four days later Roger and the rest of the band had further encouraging news when they received a letter stating they had passed a radio audition for the BBC Light programme. They had, however, barely scraped through with a four-to-three majority among the BBC's judging panel. The august Corporation's files reveal that the panel's assessment of The Who included a note that two members of the band had turned up 25 minutes late for the audition. 'With the right material and production, they could very easily make a hit' was the comment of one of the four judges who voted in favour of The Who. 'Ponderous and unentertaining' was one of the less favourable verdicts among the three who gave the band the thumbs down.

The chart entry and the BBC radio breakthrough were

heartening, especially as The Who had previously failed their first BBC audition almost a year before. It was important, too, for the wider exposure they required. At that time there were no commercial radio stations and so the BBC had a monopoly on what music was broadcast to the nation.

Roger scanned the music press eagerly for signs that 'I Can't Explain' was becoming a really big hit. When the record climbed to number 25 there was much jubilation at a first Top 30 hit, but this quickly turned to disappointment when it dropped out of the charts completely. It was a worrying week for all concerned. 'But then I got lucky,' said Lambert.

'Sir Winston Churchill happened to die in a week when I'd managed to get The Who booked on to *Ready Steady Go!*, which was the key TV programme for launching new artists. Overnight, because of Sir Winston's death, the show was forced to switch from Studio Nine, its regular studio at Television House in Kingsway, in the West End of London, because this was now reserved for the Churchill memorial broadcast.

'Instead, *Ready Steady Go!* was moved to Studio One, a great hangar of a place out at Wembley. The result was that the show didn't have enough youngsters to make up a suitable live audience for such a vast place. Every week they hand-picked about 180 young people to make up the studio audience who would dance along to the records. Now, because of the switch due to the Churchill broadcast, this particular week they needed about 150 more. I could hardly believe my luck. "I've got my Hundred Faces," I was able to tell the producers. "You can have them."

'They quickly agreed, so suddenly I'm going around with a fistful of tickets for *Ready Steady Go!* and every single one of those tickets is going straight into the pocket or handbag of a die-hard Who fan whose name and address I knew and could therefore keep tabs on. The result was that I got dozens of them on to the show as dancers.'

Roger was elated when Lambert told him that he had managed

to get The Who an appearance on such an influential TV programme. Still more so when he learned that the audience would be packed with Who fans. *Ready Steady Go!* had been launched by the independent television company Rediffusion in August 1963 in response to the pop-music explosion in Britain. With its enticing catchphrase 'The weekend starts here', the show rapidly cornered a committed teenage audience who tuned in every Friday evening to see their favourite bands, interviews with pop stars who dropped in, new groups, latest fashions and trends, new dance moves and all that was hip and cool.

The importance to The Who of an appearance on *Ready Steady Go!* cannot be overstated. The show was breathlessly hosted by Cathy McGowan, who cleverly seemed as awestruck at meeting rock stars as might any of the millions of teenage girls tuning in, and it prided itself on being one step ahead of everything to do with style. It was an absolute must for the Mods and for them became something of a TV stronghold. By the time The Who made their first appearance, the show was being watched by three million viewers in the London area alone.

The Who's first spot on the programme was secured after its producer, Vicki Wickham, and director, Michael Lindsay-Hogg, had been impressed with the band on a visit to see them at the Marquee one night when the joint was jumping. Cathy McGowan had also seen The Who when they appeared at the Harrow Technical College Christmas Dance in 1964 and had reported back favourably. Also on the *Ready Steady Go!* bill with The Who would be, among others, the Animals, the Hollies, Donovan, Elkie Brooks, Goldie and the Gingerbreads and Rhythm and Blues Inc.

Roger passed on the good news of the *Ready Steady Go!* booking to the rest of the group, and when they all assembled at Wembley for the afternoon rehearsals, Roger understandably showed signs of nerves. But these were eased considerably by the promise from Kit Lambert that there would be dozens of committed Who fans in the audience thanks to his skilful manoeuvring of his Hundred Faces.

'It will be just like a home gig in Shepherd's Bush,' Lambert assured Roger, as the singer changed for his performance into a pair of tight-fitting black trousers and a Mod polo shirt with three small arty motifs on the front. At least the band would not have to put on a spontaneous rendering of 'I Can't Explain', because, as was customary for performers booked on the show at that time, The Who would be miming rather than performing their record live.

For that memorable night of 29 February 1965, Lambert had one extra trick up his sleeve. 'At that time, college scarves were all the rage among Mods,' he said. 'So as well as giving all those die-hard Who fans a ticket for *Ready Steady Go!*, I bought every single one of them a college scarf. Then I gave everyone instructions that when it came to The Who's appearance on the show they were to tear off their scarves and throw them in triumph at The Who. My coaching worked to perfection. They did exactly that, showering scarves at the band, which meant that The Who made by far the biggest impact on the night, even though they were bottom of the bill.

'The bosses of *Ready Steady Go!* very nearly killed me for what I'd engineered,' Lambert chortled triumphantly to the authors. 'But as the show went out live in those days, there was absolutely nothing anybody could do about it. I was helped by the *Daily Telegraph* of all newspapers, who got the whole thing wrong about the college scarves and reported that The Who had caused an upper-class riot on *Ready Steady Go!* Wonderful!'

Lambert was rewarded for his ingenuity and persistence when 'I Can't Explain' bounced back into the charts at number 23. Legend has it that when he saw it had registered enough sales to hit the charts once again, he went crazy, running down the street in Belgravia, yelling at the top of his voice: 'We've cracked it, you bastards! We've cracked it!'

Lambert's euphoria was understandable. Each morning following the release of 'I Can't Explain', he had been quick to get on the phone to badger the record company for news of how The Who's debut disc was faring. The day after the band's appearance on *Ready Steady Go!*, he hadn't needed to put in his customary call. To his immense satisfaction, one of the company's executives rang him to apologise for having underrated the record.

Encouraged by the impetus he had created on *Ready Steady Go!*, Lambert worked tirelessly to get 'I Can't Explain' further into the teen pop-buying consciousness. 'I went around to every record shop in west London,' he said, 'and if they hadn't got a copy of the record I gave them one to play all the time. I also went to every jukebox in west London and put the record on the jukeboxes and loaded them up with sixpences to ensure that "I Can't Explain" replayed ten times or more, over and over again. I went to clubs, bars and tiny little cafes full of motorbikers. Nothing was too small as long as it had a jukebox. At last we began to get results in west London, where The Who had been playing and had quite a following.

'And once you get your first hit, you can manoeuvre anything,' Lambert was able to boast with the glorious certainty of hindsight. 'So I set out to get all three TV networks simultaneously featuring "I Can't Explain".' It was outrageously ambitious, even for Kit Lambert, but with a little luck and clever manipulation he managed to pull it off. 'One group had a managerial row, so The Who were put in as a substitute on *Top of the Pops* in the "Tip for the Top" slot, which was marvellous because *Top of the Pops* had an audience of about five million. And we also managed to get into an obscure programme called *Beat Room* which starred Brenda Lee.

'In desperation, after the record had dropped out of the charts, I'd also gone out and made a film of the band for about £350 and sold it for £25 to a little magazine programme called *That's for Me*. So, in the end, there was one night when you couldn't get away from The Who on TV.

'It was like a party political broadcast!' continued Lambert, roaring with laughter. 'Whichever TV channel you turned to, there were my bug-uglies playing "I Can't Explain". I even managed to introduce the song in a film that was being made about my father on BBC2.'

As a first step to what Lambert cheerfully promised would be global domination by The Who, he craftily invited several of his old French film-student friends, by now film and TV producers and directors in Paris, to come over to London and shoot films on the fascinating new phenomenon of The Who and the Mods. 'We also gave parties stuffed with as many celebrities as we could lay our hands on, which was usually Terence Stamp, the film star brother of my partner Chris, and the improbable Russ Conway.' But even Lambert's smartest promotional efforts didn't succeed all the time. 'When *Les Mods* was due to go out to the French nation, the Americans decided to televise live a man walking in space for the first time,' he remembered ruefully. 'So absolutely no one saw *Les Mods.*'

But in Britain, Lambert's cleverly orchestrated saturation TV coverage paid quick dividends. 'I Can't Explain', having ricocheted back into the charts after seemingly heading for oblivion, eventually reached the Top Ten, peaking at number eight. To his delight and relief, Roger was able to scan the charts and find his band at last rubbing shoulders among the top sellers with the Beatles and a host of other British bands whom he had enviously seen hurtle past The Who to fame in previous months. 'I was very proud of that record,' says Roger. 'That was us, you know, an original song by Pete, and it captured that energy and that testosterone that we had in those days. It still does.'

As debut hits go, it's fair to say that 'I Can't Explain' far outshines the tame and trite 'Love Me Do' by the Beatles and 'Come On' by the Rolling Stones, which was an unremarkable version of an old Chuck Berry number.

Eventually sales of the single totalled 104,000, grossing £35,000. But by the time distributors Decca had received their £16,000 cut and a further £5,000 had been claimed by taxes, The Who, who were on a royalty payment of 2.5%, received just

£1,000. But, as their managers, Chris Stamp and Kit Lambert could claim their 40% of this sum, so Roger, Pete, John and Keith wound up with about £150 each, although Pete trousered slightly more as the A side's songwriter. It was enough for John Entwistle finally to hand in his notice at the Inland Revenue.

Anxious to follow up the success of 'I Can't Explain', The Who were soon back in the studios with Shel Talmy to record more tracks, including the new single, 'Anyway Anywhere Anyhow', for which Roger gained a rare co-writing credit with Pete when the latter asked him to add a sharper edge to the lyrics. The record enterprisingly contained elements of the kind of feedback and sonic trickery that Pete was exploring regularly in The Who's live performances. Hyped by Kit Lambert and Chris Stamp as the world's first 'pop art record', 'Anyway Anyhow Anywhere' spent 12 weeks in the British singles charts, peaking at number ten. A bonus for The Who was the decision by the producers of *Ready Steady Go!* to use the song temporarily as the show's signature tune.

The distinctive feedback on 'Anyway Anyhow Anywhere' thoroughly confused the powers that be at Decca in America when they received the tape from Talmy. 'They said I'd delivered a faulty master because there were all these strange noises on it,' Talmy recalls with amusement. 'I had to assure them that was the way it was meant to sound.' Roger thought Decca's mistaken response was extraordinarily naive. 'We said: "No, this is the noise we want. Cut it loud."'

Just because Roger had shared the writing credits with Pete for 'Anyway Anyhow Anywhere', it didn't mean that the two of them were beginning to resolve their glaring differences. Indeed the reverse was true.

While John Entwistle stayed out of the arguments, Keith Moon, like Pete, had little love for Roger and went into print saying that Roger hated him because he too had said he could not sing. Keith Altham, later to become The Who's faithful and hard-working publicist, recalls noting the animosity between Roger and Keith the very first time he met them at the Marquee. At the end of their set Moon came up to introduce himself to Altham, shook hands, then apologised that he had to go off straightaway since the lead singer was out to kill him. 'Why's that?' Altham enquired. 'Well, I told him he was a shit singer,' replied Moon. 'And sure enough,' says Altham, 'a few minutes later Roger appeared. He was looking for Moon and ready to beat the hell out of him.'

Not long afterwards Altham set up a meeting with Moon for an interview backstage at the *Ready Steady Go!* studios. He waited patiently in the canteen for the drummer, who eventually turned up late, which at least was an improvement on their previous appointment, when he had failed to show up at all. Altham could not fail to notice that the drummer was carrying a heavy sports bag. Dishevelled and wild-eyed, Moon sat down at Altham's table, then rummaged in his bag before pulling out an axe, which he then slammed down hard on the table in front of the publicist. 'What's that for?' an alarmed Altham enquired nervously. 'That's for Roger,' came the reply. 'Have you seen him anywhere?'

Altham soon saw for himself that the friction between the four members of The Who was genuine. 'You'd always find Roger back-stage in the thick of the battle verbally or physically in the early days,' he says. 'I made the mistake early on of going backstage straight after the show. Bad mistake! Daltrey would have Moon by the throat, and Townshend would be screaming at Daltrey that if he went on like this he was going to kick him out of the band. Basically, it was all because they cared about their performance. The audience out front would be giving them a standing ovation but, to them, if it wasn't perfect they weren't happy. They would fight.

'There was a lot of anger about The Who on stage in those early days – anger with each other, anger with the music, anger and frustration with the equipment. But there was an awful lot of passion too. It involved a lot of passion, and Townshend allied that with a lot of compassion in the way he wrote. The combination of the two together allowed Roger to sing songs that haven't had their equal.'

Such was the rancour between Moon and Roger, and between Roger and Pete, that Kit Lambert realised it would be touch-and-go as to whether he could keep the band together. As Roger once noted about the band members' strong personalities: 'We've got the four elements in The Who – Earth, Air, Fire and Water. I'm Pisces, John is Libra, Pete's a Taurus and Keith Moon's a Leo.'

Miraculously, the personnel of The Who was not to change for 14 years, but all four of them fought so fiercely for attention that Lambert expected the band to implode at any moment. 'The nearest it came to them splitting up in the early days,' he recounted, 'was when Roger walked offstage one night when The Who were playing over Burton's tearooms in Ealing and the group played on very well without him.

'Things got so bad between Roger and Pete that I was getting to the point where I was going to set up another group for Roger to carry on with. But then Pete Townshend very wisely said to me: "Christ! I know what will happen if we throw Roger out, I'll be the next to go." Which was quite true. He said: "Making Roger the scapegoat would only be setting it up for another scapegoat, and then it'll be me."

'This all happened when the group hated each other. It was very awkward managing them at this stage. There was a period of about a year when Pete was not only not on speaking terms with me but not on speaking terms with the group either, especially Roger.

'We'd be at a gig starting at 8.30pm, and at 8.29pm and 30 seconds there'd be a scrunch on the gravel outside the venue and a car door would open and Pete would get out completely dressed for the stage, guitar in hand, and walk straight past me and the rest of the group without a look or a word, march on stage, plug in his guitar, strike the first chord, play for an hour and 20 minutes, take his bow, unplug, get back in the car and away.'

Lambert sought to bring Roger and Pete together to resolve their differences once and for all. 'It eventually cleared up,' he remembered, 'with a row which lasted 18 hours of the most tearful and terrifying sort, at the end of which Pete got me so frightfully stoned on marijuana that I got back in my van outside, started up the ignition and, after I had been driving for 15 minutes, I realised I'd only managed to drive ten yards from Pete's house and that everything had gone bright yellow.

'I got out and started wandering around Ealing Common hoping things would stop being so yellow. Then I figured some food might help so, half laughing and half frightened, I went into an Indian restaurant to be served by yellow Indian men in bright yellow turbans and ate yellow rice and yellow curry. Then I walked around yellow Ealing Common again until some sort of normalcy returned.

'The break-up of The Who had been narrowly avoided – for now. But on one tour we did in Germany, Pete and Roger got all their money stolen and the others didn't. That very nearly led to a total split of The Who. That was a pretty bad time because neither Keith nor John offered to come up with any subsidy for the other two. So, having worked very hard for three weeks, Roger and Pete were going home empty-pocketed. And because of the difficult promoters in Germany, some of whom hadn't paid up, I had to pay Roger and Pete the sum of $20 in gold – it was the only money I'd got.'

Roger's dominance of the band took a serious shift once Pete Townshend's songwriting ability began to blossom. Vocally, Roger was at his most comfortable singing James Brown soul numbers, Motown and songs by Howlin' Wolf and Bukka White, and at first he had no idea how best to handle Townshend songs like 'Pictures of Lily' and 'I'm a Boy', which were soon to come along. He thought they were peculiar songs, and certainly nothing like the blues he really wanted to sing.

Inevitably, this change in the power structure of the group undermined the control Roger liked to exert over the others. Such was the feuding and in-fighting, Lambert considered it a major achievement to get them all together to pose for a photo for the cover of their first album, *My Generation*, released in December 1965. To stress The Who's Mod leanings and that they were, indeed, leaders of the Mod generation, they were colourfully dressed for the photo, Entwistle with a Union Jack jacket draped over his shoulders and Roger in check trousers and a powder-blue roll-neck sweater under a short blue denim jacket. And to ram home the explosive nature of the four personalities that made up The Who, Lambert had the cover photo taken at Surrey Docks in south-east London, with the quartet standing next to four oil drums containing propane.

The highlight of the album was Townshend's 'My Generation', with stuttering vocals by Roger. It was chosen as The Who's new single, released several weeks before the album, and by the time it had become a massive hit, towards the end of 1965, Roger was in effect meekly and humiliatingly on parole with The Who. To his dismay and shame, he had been kicked out of his band.

CHAPTER FIVE

SACKED

At the beginning I just couldn't get through to Pete and Roger. We really have absolutely nothing in common apart from music.

Keith Moon

One crisp winter morning Kit Lambert was pacing up and down irritably waiting for Roger Daltrey to arrive at his flat-cum-office on the ninth floor of Ivor Court. Roger was late for their meeting to discuss upcoming gigs and Lambert was not in the best of moods, frequently pausing in his stride to peer out of the window to see if the singer was in sight. Suddenly he turned apoplectic with rage.

'As I spied out of the window, I saw this filthy great Phantom V Rolls-Royce pull up,' Lambert recalled. 'In the back seat was Andrew Loog Oldham, manager of the Rolling Stones, stroking a white Persian cat on his lap and speaking on the telephone. Then, to my horror, I saw Roger Daltrey, Keith Moon, Pete Townshend and Stones guitarist Brian Jones getting out of the car.

'There were my artists, The Who, rolling around with the Stones. Horror-struck, I drew my service revolver, a huge 4.5 Colt special which my uncle had left me when he died, and confronted

Roger, Pete and Keith. "What's going on?" I said, waving the pistol in Roger's face. And Roger said: "We can't help it, Kit. Every time we press the button for your floor, it stops at the fifth, Andrew's floor."

'What Andrew Loog Oldham had been doing was watching for my boys to arrive on the bus with their lunchpacks and, just as they were about to get into the lift, he'd press the lift button so they'd end up on his floor and not on mine. Then he'd take them out for a ride in his Rolls. My artists were being hornswoggled by Andrew!

'I wondered why Roger and the rest of them were playing fast and loose with me, the boys. But I also knew this was the first indication of real success for The Who – Andrew getting out the binoculars and the telescopes to see them arrive and then pressing the lift button to barmitzvah my boys into his pad. Then the stealing starts. Pinching time. He wanted to manage my boys, because his boys, the Rolling Stones, were scared of them.'

Having ascertained the truth from Roger, willingly yielded up at the point of Lambert's gleaming, possibly loaded revolver, Lambert told him in no uncertain terms that he and Chris Stamp were the managers of his band and no one else would be. Then, still fuming, he turned his attention to the Rolling Stones manager. 'I went down to sort it out with Andrew and was ready to give him a punch on the nose. But I couldn't because Andrew was very charming, of course, and he offered me a ride in his Phantom with Mick and Keith.'

That temporarily defused the situation. But Lambert didn't forget it, and nor, apparently, did Andrew Loog Oldham give up trying to hijack Roger and The Who. 'One day,' said Lambert, 'just when Andrew expected The Who to come for a ride in his Rolls, it was me who rushed down and jumped into the car instead. Then I threw his Persian cat out of the window.'

Roger soon became used to Lambert's histrionics, though he couldn't help but admire the effort and enthusiasm with which Kit was throwing himself into pushing his band towards success. Roger, like the other band members, had a guaranteed income from Kit and Chris Stamp, but the co-managers were alarmed at how quickly the money was draining away, especially once Pete Townshend developed his trademark smashing up of guitars and amps.

'Money was pouring out on more and better equipment and pop art clothes,' said Lambert. 'It was a never-ending drain on money coming in. When I first found The Who, they were earning £12 to £15 a night for an average pub concert. I just had to make a stand on that and started asking for £30. But it wasn't easy. I heard promoters throw the telephone across the room when I asked for £30, or they'd slam the receiver down on me. It was hard going because I'd guaranteed The Who £80 a week and sometimes nothing was coming in at all.'

Just how the finances came to be plunging headlong into the red was summed up in an article in *Melody Maker* in August 1965. It detailed each of the four band members' equipment needs, claiming the group had a £50-a-month bill for repair of their gear and that each month Moon spent £100 on new drumsticks alone, plus £40 on cymbals and a further £10 on high hats.

Turning to Roger, the article continued: 'Singer Roger possesses a £500 PA system which he pays for himself on HP. His particular stage trick, apart from singing, is accompanying the wilder guitar solos with the screeching of his mike against a cymbal. An occasional bang smashes the mike. Roger's mike bill comes to £35 a week. An exuberant driver, he owns the group car (£1,000 on HP) which gets the boys to dates in dire emergencies. They contribute to the running costs but not to the car's purchase. Like the rest of the group Roger spends about £2 a week on haircuts and stage make-up. Most of his shirts are handmade and cost from £6 to £10 each.'

If this article had the influence of Kit Lambert hype written all over it, it was nonetheless true that his and Stamp's savings were rapidly being eaten up. 'It was 18 months after first finding them before we saw the first signs of true success, around Christmas 1965,' said Lambert. 'The first financial breakthrough was at Watford on New Year's Eve, which brought in £64 17 shillings and sixpence, which we lovingly shared out. John Entwistle couldn't believe it – he'd never seen so much money in his life.'

Just how near the management was coming to financial disaster was something Lambert tried to keep from The Who. Four or five times he met the bailiffs removing a desk and a £30 typewriter. At one financial crisis point, Chris Stamp took a job working on the movie *The Heroes of Telemark* to help keep the coffers from running completely dry.

Lambert also talked to Robert Stigwood about the possibility of his becoming the band's agent. 'He was one of the best package tour promoters around,' said Lambert, 'and at one point Chris and I were living on the lunches he was buying us to chat us up to get us with his agency. Eventually we realised that the big problem was that, unless you became a success in America, you didn't really have any success at all. And so our task was to bring The Who through in America.'

Among those who moved in circles close to The Who in their pomp, all agree on one thing: it was a miracle that the group stayed intact as a unit from one month to the next. Not only were the four members very different personalities, but they were quite prepared to brag publicly of their dislike of one another.

In an interview with *Disc*, Pete declared: 'We get on badly. Roger causes a lot of trouble because he is never satisfied with the sound and he is the only one who will ever speak about it. Roger is not a very good singer at all in my opinion. He has got a good act, but I think he expects a backing group more than an integrated group. I don't think he will ever understand that he will never have The Who as a backing group.'

Roger was wounded by Pete's stinging remarks. Roger counted himself a blues and rock singer and what made Pete's assessment of

his singing so painful was that deep down he knew he was strug-
gling to find a voice for the songs Pete was starting to write for The
Who. But, typical of Roger, he was not going to take Pete's salvo
lying down. He also used the music press to hit back, telling the
New Musical Express: 'Arguments? Sure we have them all the time.
That's why we get on so well. It kind of sharpens us up. We've got
explosive temperaments and it's like waiting for a bomb to go off.
We're not mates at all.'

Keith Moon, of course, had to have his say as well: 'At the beginning I just couldn't get through to Pete and Roger. We really have
absolutely nothing in common apart from music,' he told *Rave*.

While Pete's songwriting skills, fully encouraged by Kit Lambert,
began to set him yet further apart from Roger, the singer also had
to contend with the individualism of both Pete and Keith, which
began to dominate The Who's stage performances. Roger's power
and influence were being further eroded.

Coming from a film background, both Kit Lambert and Chris
Stamp were aware that The Who's visual presentation was as
important as the music. For this reason they invested in special
lighting for use at the group's live performances, and encouraged
them to put on something of a show, something for the audience
to look at as well as listen and dance to. The four egos that were
The Who needed no second bidding. They had always been rivals,
but now they were vying for attention with a hostility and a burning intensity, trying to do outdo one another with the most
eye-catching and ear-splitting antics on stage.

Pete Townshend gained a head start thanks to Keith Richards of
the Rolling Stones, whom The Who supported at a London gig
one night. The Stones were about to go on stage when Pete witnessed Keith going through a series of warm-up arm exercises,
stretching his arm high in the air over his guitar and then bringing
it sharply down again.

Pete was quick to pick up on this trick and develop it into an
exaggerated windmilling gesture, his right arm arcing in circles

over his head before chopping savagely down on the strings. It rarely failed to bring excited gasps and cheers from the audience, especially when he followed it up with an athletic jump into the air, knees pulled up tight almost under his chin. For variation he perfected a scissors kick high in the air while still managing to strike an angry power chord at the same time. Back down to earth once more, he would stamp in mazy steps around the stage before pointing the neck of his Rickenbacker at the audience with a snarl as if he were mowing down the lot of them with a machine gun. 'Bloody silly,' was Roger's initial reaction, not unexpected given the antagonism between them.

Keith Moon, who always fiercely vied with Roger when it came to attracting the girls, was not to be outdone. As success increasingly came the way of The Who, his drum kit seemed to grow in equal measure until he was perched on his stool surrounded by a mini-mountain range of skins, cymbals, tom-toms, snares and high hats. These Moon treated as weapons of attack, pounding his kit with bewildering speed and frightening percussive power. The average drummer of the day was often no more than a timekeeper, content to stay at the back in the shadows and lay down a rhythm. But Moon didn't just want to be seen: he was desperate to be noticed. It was his view that the drummer should really be positioned at the front of the stage and certainly in front of the singer. He seriously resented Roger standing in front of him and, to attract attention, he became mesmerising, flailing away like an octopus at the controls of a threshing machine, rolling off into ambitious individual drum runs but managing to return to the beat spot on.

Up against such spectacular stage dynamism from Pete and Keith, John Entwistle more or less opted out of competing for the limelight, preferring instead to dazzle with his virtuoso bass-guitar work while remaining deadpan and leaning up against his amp. He was content to stay in the shadows as the group's solid anchorman, unruffled by the competitive antics of the other three. John's steady, dependable presence earned him the nickname 'The Ox', which was to stay with him until the end. The sobriquet also provided the title of a racucous intrumental, partly written by John, which wound up as the final track on The Who's debut album, *My Generation*.

Roger, by contrast, was never going to be content to let Keith and Pete steal the show, even if he found at first he had little to offer visually. All Roger had was a tambourine and a microphone stand to work with. But he soon learned to pull the spotlight back on himself by extracting the mike from its stand and, while making exaggerated marching steps backwards, swinging it lariat-style over his head before deftly catching it as it came down from on high. Not only did he find himself having to contend with the others visually: he also became increasingly annoyed as the other three played louder and louder, making it more difficult for his vocals to be heard above them. To onlookers, it seemed at times as if Townshend was trying to stop Roger's vocals interfering with the sounds issuing from his guitar.

But The Who's vigorous visuals took on an altogether different and more violent character once Pete had accidentally smashed the tuning heads of his guitar through the ceiling of the Railway Hotel during a gig, causing the instrument to snap at the neck. It was an involuntary act precipitated by the fact that the stage was erected on beer crates, making the ceiling too low for Pete's robust enthusiasm. Pete's reaction to the mishap was one of anger and frustration and he proceeded to smash the remains of his guitar to bits while Roger, John and Keith played on.

The crowd's reaction to this totally unexpected brutal demolition was instant. As one, they went totally wild, unable to believe their eyes. Lambert could not believe what he had seen either – nor the extraordinary, electric response from the audience who went into a frenzy of excitement. Instantly he saw the chance to exploit his boys as the group who smashed up their instruments. It was a great gimmick, he decided, and urged Pete to wreak more havoc in future, especially when he had invited the odd journalist along to a gig to witness and report on the musical mayhem. Roger was none too sure about this display of auto-destruction. Ever the practical one in The Who, he initially argued that it had little to do with music.

But the word soon got around and audiences began to feel cheated if they went away from a Who gig without Townshend heaving at least one guitar over his shoulder before slamming it down on the stage floor and hammering it to pieces, or piercing the stack of amplifiers with the guitar's neck. Keith, for his part, could not resist joining in and would turn the finale into a battlefield by furiously kicking over his drum kit. As lead singer, Roger found it impossible to match Pete's and Keith's on-stage violence. He tried, but knocking over the mike stand or jamming the mike aggressively against Keith's cymbals looked tame by comparison.

Offstage, Roger felt further sidelined since Pete, rather than him, was increasingly The Who member sought out as spokesman for the group. The articulate Townshend, with his outstanding songs of teenage realism and his ambitious, forward-looking approach, was the obvious candidate when a comment or quote was needed.

'The problem in the early days,' says Keith Altham, 'was that it was Roger's band and then this monster with the huge amount of talent that was Pete took it over. You couldn't stop it, it was momentum. Roger resented his band and all the decisions being taken away from him by this fellow who was in the controlling position of writing the songs and had a brain to match. That was very difficult for Roger to come to terms with and caused a lot of the friction with Pete. They always fought. But it must be remembered that, although it seemed pretty destructive to a lot of people, it was part of their creative process.'

The rifts between Roger and the rest of the group hit a crisis in the autumn of 1965 after a few months that had been difficult for the singer in a variety of ways. In August, while travelling to Salisbury for a gig at the City Hall, Roger's Austin Westminster was involved in a collision with another car, causing damage estimated at £100 to his own car and £300 to the other. Roger continued on to the venue, shaken but not seriously hurt. Then, during the gig, some over-exuberant fans yanked his microphone stand into the crowd, and as he reached down to retrieve it, he was pulled into the sea of fans and injured his back.

A week later The Who's van was stolen in bizarre circumstances. 'Fed up with driving everyone in my Volkswagen I'd got the band a van,' said Lambert. 'It wasn't very well painted and on sunny days you could see the lettering "Billiard Tables Installed On Your Own Premises" under the words "The Who". But we never seemed to be able to get effective locks to lock the stuff up and it kept getting pinched, so we drove the van to Battersea Dogs' Home to buy a large Alsatian to take touring with us and while we were choosing the Alsatian, someone nicked the van with all the equipment.' The van was eventually found in nearby Clapham with a door and around £5,000 worth of equipment missing.

Three weeks later The Who went off to tour the Netherlands and Denmark, where one concert was halted after just a few minutes when the audience swarmed in unstoppable numbers all over the stage. In the ensuing mêlée angry fans caused £10,000 worth of damage.

It was in Denmark that the hostility between Roger and the rest reached breaking point. Roger had had enough of the way their drug use was damaging his band. Pete had by now become one of the first pop musicians to admit to using drugs and in a survey in the *New Musical Express*, Keith cheekily went so far as to list his favourite food as 'French blues'. Entwistle, harking back to those days, later admitted: 'We were complete pillheads.'

Recalling the difficulty he had had in keeping the pushers away from the band, especially from Keith, Lambert said: 'As a manager, I was always having to chase away 20 or 30 pleasant rogues who would be delighted to become chauffeur-cum-heroin pusher figure to anyone as financially successful as The Who were becoming.

They seemed to be attaching themselves to Keith and I kept shooing them away. I was so worried about it I even had a very odd clause in my contract that I could fire any of The Who's employees if they worked for me or not. It was an ever-present menace, it was always too easy to get someone hooked.'

Roger had never really joined in with Keith and Pete in their use of amphetamines after an early experiment with purple hearts had left his throat dry and he had found it difficult to sing. He could see the damage drugs were doing to the group's performances when they went on stage wrecked. 'I was the only one straight and it seemed to me that the group was falling apart,' he said.

His frustration at seeing everything he had striven for disintegrate in a druggy haze of spaced-out performances drove him into a fury. The Who was more important to him than it was to the other three. To Roger the band was everything, and it drove him mad that they appeared not to be taking it as seriously as he was. One day on tour in Denmark he seized Keith's stash and flushed it down the lavatory. The drummer went berserk and flew at Roger, who erupted into a rage and decked him. 'I got so violent about it that I almost killed Keith Moon,' Roger confessed. 'It took about five people to hold me off him. It wasn't just because I hated him, it was just because I loved the band so much and thought it was being destroyed by those pills.' For the other three, this was a Daltrey punch-up too far. They were not prepared to take any more beatings from Roger and summarily sacked him from the band. Roger was devastated, and disgusted with Pete, Keith and John.

An anxious week for Roger followed as he pondered the consequence of his actions while co-managers Kit Lambert and Chris Stamp tried to patch up the differences between the four. One solution, they decided, would be to put together another group to fit around Roger, as they believed he had a voice with a great deal to offer. Once news of Roger's sacking got around, wild rumours started circulating that Pete would ally himself with a trio called

Paddy, Klaus and Gibson. There was also speculation that Boz Burrell, from a group called Boz's People, would take over Roger's role as The Who's lead singer. Boz dismissed the idea in *Melody Maker*, explaining he didn't want to be part of such a gimmicky group.

What saved Roger from possible oblivion was the current workload of The Who and the fact that their latest single, 'My Generation' was racing up the charts. As television appearances beckoned to support the record, TV producers wanted the same singer delivering on screen the same stuttering vocals as he had delivered on the record. So Roger found himself back in the band, but to regain his place he had to eat huge helpings of humble pie. The repercussions of the crisis were to last for years. 'They kicked me out and, well, I'd do anything to stay with The Who,' said Roger. 'So I went back and let them do anything they liked to me. I took a lot of shit for a long time, but it was worth it.'

The terms of Roger's reinstatement were humiliatingly laid down at a meeting of all four Who members arranged by Kit. Roger was informed that he would be lead singer once more on condition that he go along with whatever the band wanted to do. In addition there would be no more violent tantrums, no more outbursts and no more use of aggression to get his point across. According to Townshend, Roger was contrite and accepted his fate: 'It was a lesson to all of us, if you like, that there is no need to always get your way. That the most important thing is just to stay together.'

Roger's climbdown didn't stop him shouting and screaming when he chose to fight his corner, but from now on he rarely used his fists. A decade after the fracas between Roger and Keith, Pete told the American music-trade publication *Record World*: 'Originally the group was run by the iron glove of Roger. He isn't like he was any more and hasn't been for years, but he used to be very tough in getting his own way. If he didn't he'd shout and scream and stamp and in the end he'd punch you in the mouth. We'd all got big egos in the group and none of us liked it. We all got together and politely asked Roger to leave.

'Kit Lambert intervened and said why don't you give him another chance, so we said to Roger … in the future, if you want to make a point, it's got to be done sensibly, so no more getting things done by violence. Roger said from now on he'd be Peaceful Perce and I don't think he's raised his voice since. Roger had to modify himself from the inside, which is the hardest thing to do. I think it showed how much he cared about the group.'

Roger, or Peaceful Perce as he became in a nod to his roots in Percy Road, Shepherd's Bush, knew the other three had him over a barrel and that if he lost the band he would be nothing. He had started the band and driven it forward to its current success and he realised he had to listen to what the others were saying and compromise to save his position within it. The Who was the reason he was successful and he recognised that if he didn't get back into the band and hold on to his place, he might have to return to being a sheet-metal worker until the end of his days. 'I didn't fight any more,' he said, 'at least for a couple of years.'

There were times, however, when the other members of The Who were grateful for Roger's fighting instinct and fearlessness. On one occasion in Germany when four thugs started attacking their car, Roger got out and sorted them all out.

CHAPTER SIX

MY GENERATION

Out front, Roger always epitomised the strutting macho hard man, the moodiest, the meanest of mouthpieces for those Townshend lyrics. He'd snap the words out and make them sound so hostile they bordered on venom.

Who fan Keith Cronshaw

'My Generation' started off as a slow, Chicago blues-style number for which Pete Townshend had written the lyrics in the back of a car after a meeting with Kit Lambert. Kit had urged him to come up with something that made some kind of a statement, telling him: 'Write something that will set everybody talking.'

Townshend's response was 'My Generation', an angry blast at elders and so-called betters which owed its origins to his anger and frustration at the Queen Mother's arranging for the Packard hearse he owned to be towed away by police from outside his rented flat in salubrious Ebury Street, Belgravia. The Queen Mum was regularly chauffeured past the hearse *en route* through London and took exception to the doom-laden vehicle.

Townshend laid down the basics of the song on tape recorders provided for him by Lambert to encourage his songwriting. When he first played it to Lambert, the group's co-manager was hugely enthusiastic about the lyrics' raging rant. But he felt the slow, bluesy rhythm needed beefing up. Townshend duly obliged and Lambert, and even more so Chris Stamp, saw at once its potential. They earmarked 'My Generation' for the next single and felt it could be the hit record they desperately needed to take the States by storm.

Roger, however, was unimpressed with the song, partly because he was resisting generally the early blossoming of Pete as a writer and the extra clout which that gave Pete within the band and the influence he could thereby exercise over the choice of material. It took several weeks to persuade Roger and the others that The Who should record it as Pete's writing was still largely untried and so they were wary.

Eventually, on the night of 12 October 1965, The Who assembled at IBC studios in Portland Place, central London, to record their first LP. Originally the album was to have consisted largely of R&B covers but, after the success of 'I Can't Explain' and 'Anyway Anyhow Anywhere', Lambert and Townshend were anxious to record more of Townshend's compositions. Roger was unhappy that The Who seemed to be veering still further away from the R&B he favoured but found himself outmanoeuvred.

'My Generation' was just one of the tracks produced during the intense six-hour overnight session. In all, eight Townshend songs made it on to the album and he had a hand in a ninth. Roger did, however, get a chance to show his feel for the Blues and soul with cover versions of James Brown's 'Please Please Please' and 'I Don't Mind' and Bo Diddley's 'I'm a Man'. But the standout tracks were both Townshend's: 'The Kids Are Alright' and 'My Generation'.

With Shel Talmy again at the helm, 'My Generation' swept along with furious energy through two rising key changes, Roger snarling out the words, before culminating in a 30-second shattering climax of feedback, handclaps, sonic distortion, chanting and frenetic drumming from Keith Moon. In the recording studio, John Entwistle contrived to break three bass guitars before achiev-

Rock god: Roger was elevated to iconic status at Woodstock in 1969 when the sun obligingly rose over the horizon bathing Roger in golden light just as he was singing the See Me, Feel Me refrain from 'Tommy'.

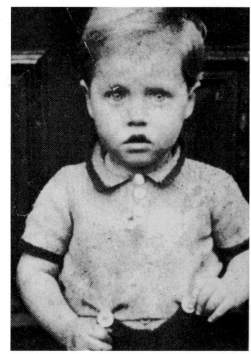

I'm a boy: Roger was evacuated from London to live with his mother on a remote farm in Scotland to escape the Blitz.

Miracle mum: Roger with his brave mother Irene Daltrey who defied the doctors who told her she would never be able to have children.

Rog the Mod: the snappy outfits so favoured by Britain's youthful Mod movement in 1966 never sat too comfortably on Roger's broad shoulders.

Ready Steady Go!: This sensational first appearance by The Who on TV's trendiest show helped propel the group's first single 'I Can't Explain' into the charts.

Rock steady: The Who became such favourites on *Ready Steady Go!* that they were invited back on to the programme as semi-regulars.

Making ripples: a promotional shot of The Who by the Serpentine in Hyde Park just as the band were starting to make an impact on the London music scene. Note Roger's fashionable flares.

A different drum: Roger turns to survey the wreckage of Keith Moon's kit after The Who's drummer had unexpectedly caused a massive explosion in his bass drum live on US TV on The Smothers Brothers' Comedy Hour in 1967. The blast blew Roger clean off his feet.

Smashing TV: Roger can't bear to look as Tommy Smothers helps Pete destroy his guitar as a finale to The Who's explosive performance. The Smothers Brothers nearly lost their jobs through Moon the Loon's unscheduled pyrotechnics.

Kitting up: Kit Lambert, right, the flamboyant, hard-living ex-public schoolboy, and Chris Stamp, co-managers of The Who. They set out to make a film about the band and ended up directing them to stardom.

Magic bus: beautiful girls were quick to jump on The Who's merry-go-round once the group had hit the big time.

ing the sound he was searching for to provide the stunning rumbling bass solo which was such a distinctive feature of the track.

The finished recording of the song finally amounted to a musically storming, lyrically belligerent, three-minutes-and-18-seconds V-sign to all and sundry, with Roger stuttering dismissively: 'Why don't you all f-f-fade away.' Townshend later admitted Roger's bristling tough-guy stance had inspired the song's attitude. 'It was the beginning of me taking on some of Roger's attributes and trying to empower myself with some of his attributes,' Pete explained. 'He had more traditional and acceptable good looks, was very tough, and didn't take shit from anybody.'

Roger, who, ironically, occasionally spoke with a stutter back in the sixties, credits Kit Lambert with coming up with the idea of stammering the word 'fade' as if he was a Mod out of his head on amphetamines and incapable of coherent speech. Lambert sidled up to Roger in the studio and suggested: 'Just try and stutter the line as though you're pilled and having difficulty in getting the words out.' Given that he had a minor impediment himself, Roger was reluctant at first but complied when Lambert told him to at least give it a try. Originally Lambert wanted Roger to employ this delivery in just one line, but the singer took it further, to telling effect, on other words, such as 's-s-sensation'.

Radio and TV producers sent advance copies of 'My Generation' gasped as they listened to it for the first time. To a man, they were struck by how Roger had, in essence, got away with singing the F-word without actually saying it. Fittingly, the explosive 'My Generation' was released as a single on Guy Fawkes Night, 5 November 1965, and first registered in the charts at number 16 before eventually rising to number two. It was kept off the top spot by, of all things, an adaptation of a Russian folk song, 'The Carnival Is Over', recorded by the harmony folk group the Seekers. 'My Generation' remains one of the best pop records never to make number one.

Predictably, the BBC banned the record, preferring to claim it was insulting to people with stammers, although they were clearly terrified at the prospect of broadcasting the unsung but palpably implied taboo word. However, the ban was eventually overturned once 'My Generation' started receiving regular airplay on the rival pirate radio stations. Sales reached 300,000 copies and inscribed The Who's name indelibly in the annals of rock music. If at that point they had downed instruments and never played another gig or made another record, 'My Generation' would still have assured The Who a place in rock 'n' roll history for having delivered the ultimate rock anthem to youth.

The sixties had produced the widest of generation gaps, and Townshend's lyrics succinctly summed up the chasm. The older generation, having survived a terrible drawn-out World War in which so many young lives were lost, were grateful to be alive. The 'My Generation' message for the teenagers of the Swinging Sixties sneeringly countered that youth was all. Living beyond it was a drag.

Quite apart from providing The Who with their biggest UK hit to date, 'My Generation' gave a resounding hint to the uninitiated as to just how explosive the band could be on stage. Teenagers catching on to The Who for the first time via 'My Generation' heard the sonic storm the band created at the climax of the song and couldn't wait to buy a ticket to see and hear them play live.

They were not disappointed. By now The Who's on-stage orgy of destruction was in full flow, and in addition Townshend was pioneering all manner of tricks to extract new, thrilling sounds from his guitar. 'They were all part of that art school tradition I'd got, of breaking the rules,' he explained. 'I was at an art school where the course was dedicated to breaking the rules and I just drafted that into my work as a guitar player. Most of the techniques I used were very virulent, violent and aggressively expressive.'

One among many thousands who became committed Who followers in this period was Keith Cronshaw, then himself a budding bass guitarist. He saw the band several times at the peak of their youthful energy, remains a fan to this day and still marvels at the sheer unrivalled musical blitz of The Who's approach, which he witnessed from just a few yards away. 'Sometimes they'd come on, maybe with Roger and Pete still arguing, and launch into what can only be described as a musical assault,' Keith remembers. 'It was like someone had lit the touchpaper, everything went up, and the last thing any of us in the audience was going to do was stand back. We were all drawn into this incredible angry noise and energy they were pumping out so powerfully.

'Townshend did things with his guitar that we music fans had never seen or heard before. He'd scrape the mike stand along the strings, or flip the toggle switch on and off to make his guitar sound like a machine gun when it was feeding back. I remember once seeing him when he was playing a Rickenbacker and apparently he'd packed it with paper so he could produce extraordinary feedback on harmonics. He'd get these amazing sounds just by waving the guitar at various points in front of the amps. It was electrifying in every sense, a fantastic frenzy of feedback fury.

'Out front, Roger always epitomised the strutting macho hard man, the moodiest, the meanest of mouthpieces for those Townshend lyrics. He'd snap the words out and make them sound so hostile they bordered on venom. Behind him Moon, like a mad Banshee, whirled away with his sticks at bewildering speed. Even in his earliest days, Moon had a 16-piece set and produced thunderous around-the-kit rolls and sizzling cymbal work while John Entwistle simply stood back and kept everything together. They were a group apart, pure originals, but when The Who sang "The Kids Are Alright" that gave all of us in the audience an identity with them.

'The auto-destruction at the end of some of their gigs was awesome, Pete ramming his guitar through the amps, spinning it high in the air and letting it crash to the floor. Then he'd pick it up again by the neck and hammer the body repeatedly into the floor as if he was trying to crush a cockroach. Meanwhile Roger would be whirling the mike stand over his head, then spearing it into Keith's kit, Moon beaming maniacally through the fog from the smoke bombs detonated inside his drums, then viciously booting his kit off stage. At the end the stage, with its splintered guitars, twisted mike stands, wrecked amps still whirring and buzzing, holes gaping in the demolished drum kit, looked as though it had taken a direct hit from a military missile. It was as though they had a war to fight and they were fighting it in front of us. And we, the audience, were loving every incredulous minute of this musical mayhem.'

It was performances like these which drew fans like Keith Cronshaw to sell-out gigs by The Who up and down the country. In the UK the success of 'My Generation' meant The Who could now command a fee of £300 a night, but Lambert and Stamp still invariably found themselves out of pocket after all the bills had been paid. New equipment didn't come cheap.

Although the album, also called *My Generation*, reached number five in the LP charts, it is only with the passage of time that its revolutionary significance has been recognised. Now it is rightly regarded as a classic, sometimes described as the first punk album.

The major disappointment for Roger, and all concerned with The Who, was the failure of 'My Generation' to make much of a dent in the American singles charts. It reached number 74 in the Billboard Hot 100, which was a fair reflection of the minimal promotion Decca accorded the record. 'The Who?' reflected one Decca marketing man at the time. 'We just thought: strange name, strange noise, strange group.'

In desperation Chris Stamp flew to New York to try to drum up some real enthusiasm, but he knew it was not going to be easy. Unlike the UK, America had no army of Mods to latch on to The Who, and the group's image was out of synch with the kind of fans who had given such a welcome to 'safe' groups from Britain like Herman's Hermits and the Dave Clark Five.

When another Townshend song, 'I'm a Boy', was released in the States in December 1966, this again made no impact on the charts, although it reached number two in the UK. The song presented Roger with a new challenge: how to interpret Pete's lyrics about a young boy aggrieved that his parents really wanted him to be a girl. Eventually he decided to try to sing it as a bewildered eight-year-old might do.

A new LP, *A Quick One*, released in December 1966, repeated the divisive transatlantic pattern – it reached number four in the UK album charts but failed to register strongly in the US. A collection of songs of variable quality, it left The Who's R&B influence well behind. But it did at least allow Roger to sing in his preferred comfort zone on a cover version of Martha and the Vandellas' 'Heatwave'. And the nine-minute 'A Quick One While He's Away' was Townshend's first mini-opera, a hint at the glory that was to come with *Tommy*.

CHAPTER SEVEN

AMERICA

Don't ask me to be a good boy because I'm out there in a rock 'n' roll band.

Roger Daltrey

It was May 1967 before America finally woke up to The Who, and when they did so it was – bizarrely – to 'Happy Jack', one of Pete Townshend's stranger compositions. A novelty song about a tinker on the Isle of Man tormented by local kids, 'Happy Jack' was inferior by far to 'I Can't Explain', 'Anyway Anyhow Anywhere' and 'My Generation', all of which had failed to set the US charts alight. 'Happy Jack', although unrepresentative of what The Who were really about, nonetheless gave the band a first foothold in the US charts by reaching number 24.

No one was more surprised than Roger when the Americans started buying 'Happy Jack' in sizeable enough quantities to turn it into a hit. When first presented with the song by Pete, he had absolutely no idea how he was going to go about singing it. His first reaction was that it sounded like a German oompah-band song. Later he decided it was more like a ditty that Burl Ives, the American folk singer famous for singalong rhymes for children, would sing and so he gave it a Burl Ives treatment.

'Happy Jack' now paved the way for The Who to capitalise on belated US recognition. And if Roger had ever doubted he would achieve real success in his career in music, it was setting foot in America that made him realise he really had made it in his chosen profession. Ever since he had quit his factory job, Roger had never harboured any thoughts of being anything other than a singer. But to fly into New York to hear The Who finally had a hit with 'Happy Jack', and to turn on the radio and hear disc jockeys at last enthusing over 'I Can't Explain', 'My Generation' and 'Substitute', was confirmation for Roger that he really had arrived.

It gave him tremendous satisfaction to be taking The Who's music to the country whose early rockers like Presley, Buddy Holly and Eddie Cochran had first inspired him to take up the guitar and become a rock singer himself.

The Who were, in fact, very late starters when it came to joining the invasion of the States by British groups, a trail first blazed several years earlier by the Beatles and the Rolling Stones. And Roger could be excused for thinking that it was high time his lot joined the party. By the time The Who arrived in New York in the spring of 1967, a whole host of British groups far less musically capable than The Who had already toured with great success and had topped the American pop charts.

Chart-toppers from the UK included the Troggs, the Dave Clark Five, Wayne Fontana and the Mindbenders and Herman's Hermits. The last of these had even managed to reach number one in the States, first with 'I'm Henry VIII, I Am', a cockney music-hall number dating back to 1911, and then the vaudeville-style ditty 'Mrs Brown, You've Got a Lovely Daughter'. The Beatles, moreover, had notched up no fewer than 32 Top 40 hits in America and the Rolling Stones 14 by the time 'Happy Jack' put The Who on the map.

Now The Who were at last in America for their first stage

appearances as one of a string of acts booked by the disc jockey Murray Kaufman. Known as Murray the K and fond of styling himself 'the fifth Beatle', the DJ had booked The Who for show-cases at the RKO 58th Street Theater for his ten-day Easter show 'Music in the 5th Dimension'.

Also on the bill were Mitch Ryder, Wilson Pickett, the Blues Magoos, Smokey Robinson and Cream, but Murray the K knew he had something special in store with The Who when Pete turned up for rehearsals in a suit sporting battery-operated lights which blinked on and off and proceeded to smash up his guitar.

'They had to play five to seven concerts a day,' said Lambert, 'starting at ten in the morning. It was a gruelling schedule, but we had doctors standing by with vitamin shots to keep them going. The support was much more like the support you get at a football match. They'd play with no applause and no screams at all, and then in the very last number the whole audience would riot. It was very disturbing, playing to a dead audience for an hour and then I'd have to rush on stage and throw people back into the audience to stop the boys being torn apart.'

Audiences who had heard of The Who's reputation for butcher-ing their equipment were not disappointed. The group's on-stage devastation during the ten-day run put paid to more than 20 microphones, five guitars, four speaker cabinets and a ten-piece Premier drum kit – which left Lambert tearing his hair out and roadie Bob Pridden desperately working overtime trying to glue the remnants together after each show. Roger broke every micro-phone he was given save for Murray the K's own personal gold-plated mike. Wisely, he left that one intact.

'At one point later on, I had standing orders with just about every guitar shop in the US,' said Lambert. 'They were for Fender guitars, which would have to be flown all over the States as the group toured to keep up with the pace. I owned almost every gui-tar in America at one stage.

'It became a bore quite frankly for the group that audiences felt dissatisfied unless they broke up their equipment. But I didn't dare tell The Who that by then there were 37 other groups doing the same, not to mention the dirty little Yardbirds had started to play in Union Jack jackets.'

It was during one of The Who's appearances on a Murray the K show in America that Roger caught the eye of a tall, willowy and vivacious auburn-haired model called Heather Taylor. She was modelling clothes on the same show and Roger was immediately attracted to her, still more so when they got chatting and he discovered that, despite her American accent, Heather had been born in Hammersmith Hospital and had spent her early childhood living just a few streets away from the Daltreys before her family moved to Connecticut.

Just a few weeks later, after The Who had returned to England and played a gig at the Marquee in London, Roger was surprised and excited to bump into Heather again at the trendy Speakeasy Club in the West End, where she was enjoying a night out with a group of friends. As a successful model, Heather had met plenty of famous men and was unfazed by the cocky young singer with The Who. Over the next few months, while staying in touch with Roger, she patiently stayed in the background while he proceeded to date various other girls she knew, including one who was a good friend of hers.

With so many girls throwing themselves at Roger, Heather was wise enough not to chase him. By the time Roger had finished squiring a succession of her friends, he finally homed in on Heather and was ready to embark on a meaningful relationship with her. 'It took me six months to realise I really liked Heather,' Roger remarked. And by then Heather knew exactly what she was in for. 'I knew his reputation and what to expect,' she said, adding: 'If you have a reputation like Roger's, that works for women. You get excited by it, and interested in the man.'

Heather was undeniably beautiful, but Roger was not just enamoured of her sex appeal. At a time when Women's Lib was starting to become a highly vocal movement, Roger was struck by how ultra-feminine and level-headed Heather appeared. This appealed to him enormously. 'I do what I want to do, and she does what I say,' was how Roger once described their relationship. 'And I agree that's the best way,' said Heather.

Eventually, as their affair became more intimate and passionate and showed signs of permanency, Heather moved into the flat Roger had by now acquired in St John's Wood with his rewards from The Who. 'That seemed so swanky at the time,' Heather recalled. 'But although Roger was earning £1,000 a week, it was costing him £1,500 to pay for the equipment they smashed up on stage. So, although we weren't exactly poor, he just had a flashy car, a bed and no furniture.'

After his first experience of marriage, Roger was in no rush to wed again. Heather, on the other hand, recognised she had met the man she wanted to marry and the subject of marriage was frequently raised over a period of four years before Roger finally decided to take the plunge again. Many years later he was able to say: 'My marriage is successful because firstly I was very lucky in finding the right woman, and secondly I was very honest about who I was and what my job was when I married Heather.

'The only reason to get married is to have children and she wanted to have children. I thought, I'll marry you. But you know what job I'm in. Don't ask me to be a good boy because I'm out there in a rock 'n' roll band .' Despite the disruptions threatened by his lifestyle, Roger was determined to work at his marriage. 'If you're honest,' he said, 'you can keep anything together. You have to fight for it, though. People give up too easily. We also have great sex, which helps.'

With The Who enjoying ever-greater success, Roger and Heather moved to a beautiful fifteenth-century cottage at Hurst, in the Berkshire countryside, which he set about renovating whenever he managed to find the time. Roger had lived in London all his life, but now his eyes were opened to the simple delights of the countryside and he revelled in his new rural surroundings. He enjoyed going for country walks with Heather and sitting in front of a roaring log fire in a cottage steeped in 400 years of history. The nights when he would drive his Corvette up to London to hit the clubs became fewer and fewer. It was during this period of cosy domesticity in 1970 that Roger, who was then 26, finally decided he and 22-year-old Heather should get married.

The couple opted for a low-key wedding ceremony conducted in the local register office, but decided that the reception should be on a grand scale and invited 400 guests to share in the celebrations. As well as making plans with Heather to lay on a sumptuous feast, Roger spent the day before the wedding organising the setting-up of a funfair for the guests. Sited in a nearby field, this included coconut shies, whelk stalls and hot-dog stands.

It should have been the perfect day, but when the couple pre-sented themselves at the registry office, they were shocked to find that they were unable to be joined in matrimony. They were informed they could not wed that day as Roger's divorce from his first wife Jacqueline was not yet finalised.

With 400 guests heading for their wedding party, Roger and Heather were in the most difficult quandary. Eventually they thought it would be impossible, not to mention unfair, to change at short notice the travelling plans of 400 people and that it was best to go ahead with the celebrations. But they resolved to tell none of the guests that they had not, in fact, tied the knot as planned. 'It was the most amazing wedding reception – without a wedding – you've ever seen,' said Roger.

Heather and Roger, and the registrar, managed to keep the non-marriage a secret and the couple kept up the pretence in front of their guests. There was nothing to suggest to anyone else that they had not just wed. Six weeks later, on 19 July 1971, Roger and Heather quietly went off to the registry office in Battle, East Sussex, an area where they had recently been house-hunting, and officially became man and wife. Steve Ellis, singer with the group

Love Affair, was one of the witnesses there to ensure that this time the couple were well and truly married.

As he kissed his bride, Roger pondered how strange it was that he could travel around the world and end up marrying a girl from just a few streets away. His choice of wife met with the full approval of his parents. 'Heather's very down to earth, but she could entertain the Queen,' Roger's mother remarked.

When Roger met Heather during The Who's first incursion into America, back in 1967, Keith Moon was discovering the dubious art of rearranging the furnishings and fittings of hotels. The band were originally booked into the upmarket Drake Hotel on 55th Street but their irresponsible behaviour soon saw them switched to the less swanky Gorham Hotel nearby. And it was here that Moon is said to have lit the fuse to his first hotel bomb in protest at John Entwistle blasting away on trumpet practice in the room next door.

Moon's laying waste of hotel rooms was to become legendary, and hugely costly, and although Roger was never averse to having fun on the road, such wanton destroying of TV sets, furniture, fittings and cars was something he increasingly distanced himself from in the years to come.

For a start, Roger was a couple of years older than the other members of The Who, and he was a war baby who could remember post-war rationing when food, provisions and luxuries were limited and luxuries hard to come by. His family background had instilled in him that possessions and achievements were something you worked to attain and, once won, were to be cherished rather than demolished. They were far too precious simply to smash up. That, to Roger, seemed madness.

In between the determined assault on America and a hectic schedule of live appearances back in the UK, The Who managed to find the time to finish recording their third album, *The Who Sell Out*, which came out in November 1967 and is now regarded by many as one of the great rock albums of the era and the one that at last began to fully define Roger's role within the group.

The album was chock full of story-telling songs by Pete Townshend, and Roger was able to inhabit the various characters these threw up and develop the dramatic feel he was later to bring to his vocals for the rock opera *Tommy*.

The Who Sell Out drew The Who as near as they possibly dared to jumping on the psychedelia bandwagon that became so fashionable for groups during and after 1967's 'Summer of Love'. The highlight of the album was 'I Can See for Miles', which remains a favourite of Roger's and is, in his view, one of the best-produced tracks The Who ever made. Almost a full day was spent in the studio painstakingly putting down layer upon layer of harmonies for the song.

The LP was a concept album, Townshend's homage to the pirate radio stations which had served The Who so well by promoting their records. That August the pirate stations, so beloved in the sixties, had just been blown out of the water by the Marine Broadcasting Bill, which made them illegal. At first the idea had been to punctuate *The Who Sell Out* with commercials between the songs, but this was abandoned in favour of including some real Radio London jingles and some humorously concocted spoof commercials of The Who's own making, extolling the virtues of acne cream, deodorant, a body-building course, baked beans and a car showroom. The album is still one of Roger's favourites, both for its sense of humour and for its Who trademark of holding two fingers up to the establishment.

The cover design by David King and Roger Law, the second later to become one of the creators of TV's satirical puppet show *Spitting Image*, featured each member of The Who in an outrageous pose for a 'commercial'. Pete was photographed stripped to the waist holding a giant deodorant stick to his armpit, while Keith applied a tube of cream to his spotty face. John Entwistle, posing as a one-time weakling but now a muscle man thanks to a Charles

Atlas course, was pictured in an animal skin holding a teddy bear with a blonde in a bikini draped around him.

Originally, Roger was to have been the muscle man. But instead he was forced to take on the unpleasant task of being photographed in a bath full of baked beans, satirically promoting 'a cowboy's breakfast', after John contrived to be late for the photo session so he would get the girl and Roger would be lumbered with the beans.

Roger definitely drew the short straw, as for him the photo shoot at photographer David Montgomery's studio in Edith Grove, Chelsea, amounted to an uncomfortable hour posing for the camera in the bath, freezing-cold baked beans almost covering him. Huge cans of them, brought directly from cold storage, were emptied into the bath around Roger, leaving him shivering and complaining loudly how icy he felt, all the more so because the group had just come back from Hawaii. Moon sympathetically set up an electric fire behind the bath, but to little avail. All it did was warm up Roger's back, which made him feel even colder everywhere else. 'One half of me was cooking, my feet were freezing and it made me very ill,' Roger remembers. 'I did actually get pneumonia. I was ill for a very long time.'

Roger and the rest of the band were desperate for *The Who Sell Out* to become a big hit. Quite apart from anything else, they all needed the money. At the end of their first tour of the US supporting Herman's Hermits, they had grossed $40,000 but ended up returning home $5,000 in debt. Any profit they had hoped for had been eroded by the cost of replacing smashed equipment, travel expenses and general over-indulgence while on the road.

Keith Moon was personally landed with a bill of $24,000 after his riotous twenty-first birthday, which has passed into legend as the epitome of rock misbehaviour. He wound up spending a few hours in jail after a Lincoln Continental ended up in the swimming pool of the Holiday Inn in Flint, Michigan, and the local sheriff took exception to being hit by the best part of several tiers of marzipan and icing sugar from the drummer's birthday cake. Generously, many of the cake-spattered guests and the other three members of the band stumped up to help pay Moon's gigantic bill for the damage caused. It says much about The Who's parlous financial state at the end of the tour that Entwistle had to borrow $100 for the air ticket back to England.

Recounting the band's money woes to the *Observer*, Roger said: 'When we had our first hit, "I Can't Explain", we started earning what was then pretty good money, say £300 a night. But after the first year we were £60,000 in debt. The next year, after working our balls off, we were £40,000 down. The biggest choke of all came a year after that when we found we were back up to £60,000 again. Every accountants' meeting was ridiculous. We always owed so much money that we ended up rolling around the floor, laughing ourselves silly.'

Within months, riding on a growing reputation and their hit records, The Who were welcomed back to America in June 1967 in resounding fashion. After playing at the famous Fillmore auditorium in San Francisco, they were lined up for the most ambitious rock festival yet mounted, the three-day Monterey International Pop Festival.

This was the Summer of Love, when a growing army of hippie flower children in flowing kaftans preached 'peace and love, man'; when San Francisco's Haight–Ashbury district became a mecca for the young idealists who smoked pot and sought to bring a peaceful new order to a troubled world. Singer Scott McKenzie encapsulated the movement in song with his big hit 'San Francisco (Be Sure to Wear Flowers in Your Hair)'.

At The Who's two Fillmore gigs, the hippies were first jolted out of their gentle stoned state by Townshend's crunching opening chords and then scared out of their stupor by the band's customary rampaging performance and omni-wrecking finale. 'We were waging a class war and they were waging a peaceful protest against Vietnam,' observed Roger. 'We really just didn't understand one another. They wanted peace and love and got anger and resentment. They were not quite ready for the 'orror that was the 'Oo!'

Next, The Who's musical typhoon roared on to Monterey, where again their reputation was enhanced by a shattering performance which left the crowd spellbound. But how different it all might have been had Jimi Hendrix not been deprived of the chance to perform before The Who.

Tempers had flared backstage when Roger and Pete learned that Hendrix planned to go on stage and wind up his set with a Who-style guitar-wrecking spree. Townshend, in particular, was incensed that Hendrix was intending to appropriate this special effect and steal his thunder. He knew that if The Who went on after Hendrix and administered their customary mayhem to their equipment, they would seem like copycats rather than originators. A fierce argument ensued, eventually settled amicably by the toss of a coin, which let The Who choose to go on before Hendrix.

The assembled throng might have known what was coming when Eric Burdon, lead singer with the Animals, announced The Who with the words: 'This band will destroy you … in more ways than one.'

Burdon was right. The bead-laden, flower-bedecked hippies watched open-mouthed as Roger, wearing a multicoloured table cloth picked up in the King's Road, Chelsea, and made into a shawl, tore into 'My Generation' as the climax to the set. At the end Townshend administered a fearful hammering to his guitar on the floor of the stage while Moon kicked his kit vehemently into the press pit. A moment of stunned disbelief engulfed the crowd before they broke into huge applause.

It was a pivotal moment in The Who's winning over of America, though Roger's preferred memory of the event was the jam session in the dressing room under the stage that preceded their set. Hendrix was standing on a chair and running through his extraordinary repertoire of guitar tricks while playing along to tracks from the Beatles' just-released *Sergeant Pepper* album. Among those joining in this impromptu session were Janis Joplin, Brian Jones of the Rolling Stones, Mama Cass of the Mamas & the Papas, as well as Townshend and Moon. 'It was better than any of the things on the show,' Roger reflected. 'It was amazing, just a shame no one was there to record it.'

The Who's stunning performance at Monterey did their reputation in America a power of good and the film of the festival further helped to spread the word. Soon they were touring the country, absurdly as support for Herman's Hermits, who were by now massively popular in the States. The largely pre-pubescent fans and their mums who flocked to see that cheeky Herman boy – Peter Noone – with the endearing crooked-tooth smile were given the shock of their lives when The Who came on as the warm-up band. As Roger snarled his angry lyrics at the audience, Pete, John and Keith blitzed them with their instrumental power. As word spread, more and more tickets for future gigs were snapped up by The Who's rapidly expanding US fan base. Humiliatingly for Herman's Hermits, the venues would half-empty once The Who completed their set.

The Monterey Festival also led indirectly to The Who's now legendary explosive television appearance which saw Roger literally blown clean off his feet and Pete Townshend left deaf for 20 minutes. The festival had been compered by Tommy Smothers, one half of the Smothers Brothers, formerly folk satirists who had progressed on the back of the beat boom to become hosts of CBS's popular variety show *The Smothers Brothers' Comedy Hour*. Having seen at first hand the reaction to The Who at Monterey, Tommy snapped them up for a guest TV appearance.

The Who were booked to appear along with two Hollywood greats, Mickey Rooney and Bette Davis, and all appeared to be going smoothly during rehearsals for an evening taping of the show. After a bit of prearranged banter with Tommy Smothers, the group were to perform 'I Can See for Miles' and 'My Generation'.

The second number was to climax with a closely controlled

version of the usual instrument-smashing and a smoke-producing explosion from inside Keith Moon's bass drum. Rehearsals were conducted under the eagle eye of the TV company's fire marshal, who allowed just the tamest of explosions and the minimum of effects from the smoke bomb. It was all far too tame for Moon's liking, and in between rehearsals and the broadcast he started hitting the brandy and bribing the fire marshal with fat dollar bills to allow him to pack a greater explosive charge inside his kit. Eventually the sum of $300 cleared the way for Moon to install four times the permitted amount of explosive in his bass drum. Come the finale, with millions watching, Pete stood in front of the drum riser and heaved his guitar one more time over his shoulder, ready to smash it to bits, when the bass drum suddenly blew up with a shattering bang like a thunderclap.

The force of the blast blew Moon off the riser and knocked Roger flat on his face. At the same time Townshend's hair stood on end and caught fire. When the dust began to settle and the smoke to clear, the precise extent of the damage became evident. Townshend had temporarily lost his hearing and was banging his head with his hand in an effort to regain his hearing and ensure his hair was no longer alight. Moon was sitting at the back with a triumphantly mad grin on his face but nursing a nasty cut on his arm. His magnificent detonation had caused part of a cymbal to shear off and the shrapnel had sliced into his arm. Not for nothing did Moon later have the words 'Keith Moon, Patent British Exploding Drummer' inscribed on his Premier kit. The postscript to this extraordinary piece of live television was Tommy Smothers walking through the debris, around his neck an acoustic guitar, which Townshend, still a shade unsteady on his feet, removed and stomped into shreds.

Mickey Rooney, watching the pyrotechnics from the wings, thought this wholly unexpected TV earthquake was hilarious. He roared with laughter, clapped his hands and called for more. The reaction from Bette Davis was altogether different. Dolled up in an

Elizabethan costume ready for her appearance, she fainted clean away into Rooney's arms.

For The Who it had been a lucky escape. The physical damage could have been catastrophic. The Smothers Brothers nearly lost their TV show over the incident, but for The Who it brought still wilder interest from American youth, reflected in encouraging sales of their records. By the autumn of 1967 'I Can See for Miles' had reached number nine in the US charts, one place higher than it had achieved in the UK. For Pete Townshend this was a bitter pill to swallow. 'To me it was the ultimate Who record yet it didn't sell. I spat on the British record buyer,' he said. So upset was he at the lukewarm response to what he considered his masterwork that he seriously feared The Who were finished.

Of the four members of the group, it was Roger who drew the most satisfaction from seeing that, with 'I Can See for Miles' in the Top Ten, The Who's conquest of America had more than begun. But it would take an appearance at the epochal Woodstock festival and the birth of a boy called Tommy to finally win The Who parallel status in America with the Beatles and the Stones as one of the greatest rock bands in the world.

CHAPTER EIGHT

WOODSTOCK

Tommy *was huge. It made Roger into a proper frontman.*
He was magnificent on stage from this time forwards. I felt
as if a huge weight had been lifted.

Pete Townshend

A dozen hit singles for The Who in less than four years had
kept the band at the forefront of British rock. But 1968 proved
a disastrous year as a result of a chaotic, incident-riddled tour of
Australia and New Zealand and the failure of two singles,
'Dogs' and 'Magic Bus', to make the UK Top 20 for the first
time.

Successful singles were vital to sustaining the band's high profile, but suddenly their offerings were not selling any more. No
one was more alarmed than Pete. He felt The Who were now
being eclipsed by the likes of the supergroup Cream and the
guitar genius Jimi Hendrix, that The Who sat very uncomfortably with the new psychedelic era and that the band could not
be classed as experimental like Pink Floyd. He recognised that
the way to salvage The Who was to change his approach to
songwriting.

Encouraged by Kit Lambert, Pete now looked to expand his

composing talents way beyond a string of three-minute songs. Lambert made it clear to the band that modern pop music didn't have to be just three minutes of vinyl containing a song with a catchy hook and a middle eight. He hated the idea of rock being belittled in some way or looked down on by classical enthusiasts. He was not ashamed to say he was proud of rock 'n' roll, but there was no doubt that he wanted it to be accepted as an art form in its own right. And while the group's co-manager was respectful of the importance of the three-minute single, he had grander plans. To this end, he provided Pete with two good-quality tape decks on which to work and guided him towards the idea of a big rock opera.

Despite being the son of the lauded composer Constant Lambert, Kit didn't balk at stating that classical opera had become too elitist and that he saw no reason why rock should not have its own equivalent. 'I kept driving Pete on to come up with something which used operatic techniques,' he said.

Happily for Townshend and The Who, Lambert's call for something grand coincided with Pete's discovery of Meher Baba, an Indian yogi whose teachings about a higher spiritual awareness had a profound effect on him. Urged on by Lambert's faith in his abilities to write a rock opera, Pete came up with *Tommy*, a loose story about a deaf, dumb and blind boy who becomes a fantastic pinball player and regains his senses through a spiritual awakening. Such an outlandish concept was not easy to sell to his bandmates, especially Roger with his natural leanings towards R&B and rock 'n' roll, but with Lambert enthusiastically throwing his weight behind the project and even contributing a working script, Pete pressed on with a series of demos. It was an insular business and the other members of the band simply decided the best thing was to let Pete get on with it.

It was a painstaking process. 'When we did *Tommy*, Pete used to come in some days with just half a demo,' Roger remembers. 'We used to talk for hours, literally. We probably did as much talking as we did recording. We spent weeks sorting out arrangements for the music.'

But gradually Pete's rock opera took shape and recording finished in March 1969, just as 'Pinball Wizard', the scene-setting single from the double album, took The Who back into the UK charts, where it peaked at number four.

When *Tommy* was given a big press launch at Ronnie Scott's club in London on 1 May 1969, reviews were mixed, one of the leading music weeklies describing it as 'sick' and 'pretentious'. But there were also encouraging notices from such celebrated classical composers as William Walton and Leonard Bernstein.

Roger, and even more so Pete, were aware that *Tommy*'s success would hinge on live presentation of the rock opera and the group rehearsed extensively and refocused their energies until they were satisfied they had developed a stage act to match the record. Then, one week after the launch of *Tommy*, The Who embarked on their first US headlining tour, playing large sections of the opera to huge and appreciative audiences at venues that grew ever bigger as promoters began to cotton on to the sheer scope and innovative scale of the work.

It was around this time that Roger, with the help of a photographer cousin, devised a new image for himself. By his own admission, he had always been a rocker trying to compete in a Mod's uniform, but now at last he felt it was time he was allowed to be himself. He grew his hair long, into a mass of curls, and from a friend who made buckskin outfits he ordered a buckskin suit with long tassels dangling from the arms. When Keith Moon opened a magazine and saw a picture spread of the new-style Roger, he yelled 'Yuk' and wrote the word in large letters across the pages. But, with the jacket worn open to reveal Roger's lean frame, it was an image which evoked anything but this response from the singer's fans. Roger may have been Tommy on stage, but he was now transformed into a rock god before their eyes.

'He went from tough muscled frontman of The Who to angel

with curly hair,' says Keith Altham. 'That was down to his photographer cousin, and it fitted Tommy to a T. There was a time when that androgynous image of the slim, snake-hipped rock star, which Jagger had invented, disappeared and became synonymous with the rejection of the drug culture. And it was like Keep Fit time, be healthy, be fit, be attractive and that was something Roger fell into line with very quickly. It was something that appealed to him because he wasn't into the drugs or the androgynous look. There was never any doubt what gender Roger was.'

While British fans were quick to take to *Tommy*, eventually pushing it to number two in the UK album charts, the record made much slower progress in America. But, just as *Tommy* looked to be stalling there, The Who played Woodstock and enjoyed a pivotal moment of supreme timing and good fortune which they could not have engineered in their wildest dreams.

It's a supreme irony that, having worked so hard to win over America, The Who finally achieved it through a filmed stage performance at the world's greatest pop festival when they were all desperately tired, deprived of sleep, out of their heads on LSD, angry and annoyed at being kept waiting, and finally playing what Roger believes was the worst Who gig of them all. Asked to make use of clapped-out speakers, the band produced a sound that Roger can only describe as 'absolutely dire'.

This unlikely turning point in The Who's American fortunes occurred at what was formally named the Woodstock Music and Art Fair, a three-day event held at Bethel, in upstate New York, in mid-August 1969. Against his better judgement, after a particularly gruelling tour stretched way beyond the two months originally scheduled, Pete Townshend agreed The Who would play at Woodstock.

The Who were originally scheduled to appear at the festival on the evening of Saturday, 16 August 1969, but they were kept waiting for some 12 hours before going on stage in the early hours of Sunday. By this time they were suffering desperately from lack of sleep and from the fact that almost everything available backstage to drink and eat had been liberally spiked with LSD. In effect, they had been tripping for almost 12 hours. They were in no fit state to stand up in front of anybody, let alone the estimated 450,000 restless and expectant music fans by now packing the festival site.

There was further aggravation and further delay when it looked as though The Who would not be paid their agreed appearance fee of $12,500. While all sides sought a way around this impasse, the Woodstock organisers tried to force The Who into taking the stage by threatening to announce to the fans that the band had cancelled because they had not been paid. When it became apparent that this attempt at blackmail would fail, the fee was finally paid.

It was in this tense, LSD-laced, angry and argumentative climate that Roger, Pete, Keith and John finally walked on stage in the early hours of the morning to give a performance which was further undermined by a huge overworked PA system that gasped and threatened to breathe its last at any moment. 'It was a miserable experience because I couldn't perform my best,' says Roger. 'By the time we got on stage we were in no condition whatsoever to play a show.'

The confusion the tripped-out foursome felt on taking to the stage was also compounded by their finding the stage swarming with film crews assigned to capture the festival on celluloid for a movie of the event. Pete tried to disperse them with a well-aimed boot. More drama unfolded when immediately after they had played 'Pinball Wizard', a Yippie activist by the name of Abbie Hoffman chose to invade the stage, grab hold of a mike and launch into a speech denouncing the ten-year jail sentence for the leader of the militant White Panthers, John Sinclair. Pete Townshend decided that such an interruption to The Who's set was not only downright discourteous but that a music festival was not the place for an unscheduled political speech. For his pains, Hoffman duly received a swatting from Townshend's guitar, which sent him sprawling into the photographers' pit.

Out of all this chaos, The Who somehow managed to emerge with enough energy and well-drilled expertise to retrieve the situation, for the huge crowd began to warm to their performance.

And then it happened – a moment of luck and timing which probably changed the lives of Roger and the other members of The Who for ever.

Just as Roger was launching into the 'See Me, Feel Me, Touch Me, Heal Me' refrain from *Tommy* – one of Townshend's simplest and most resonant tunes – the sun stole over the horizon, bathing the stage with the first golden shafts of dawn light. It was a remarkable, magical instant, the timing of which was not lost on the crowd, who were by now extremely appreciative. Or on Roger, who says of that moment: 'The fact the sun came up on the "See Me, Feel Me" bit was extraordinary. It really was like a gift from God.' The huge congregation of flower children, not long risen from their slumbers, thought likewise.

That truly golden moment ensured that The Who were one of the sensations of the legendary Woodstock festival and contributed greatly to establishing them in America as one of the world's greatest rock bands. Despite Roger's insistence that, on a musical level, this really was the worst gig they ever played, the subsequent movie also, ironically, confirmed Roger's status as a new rock god. During The Who's appearance the cameras tended to focus long and hard on Roger, often capturing him in slow motion, cavorting, bobbing and weaving, tossing his head full of curls as the sun's first fingers of light reached out to him.

By the time Roger and the rest of the band flew back to the UK to appear at the Isle of Wight festival, with Bob Dylan among others, two weeks later, sales of *Tommy* had reached half a million. The album eventually reached number four in the US album charts, where it resolutely stayed for 50 weeks and, with the possible exception of the Rolling Stones, The Who were now the greatest live band in the world. *Tommy* had provided them with a wealth of dramatic new material and now they were the hottest attraction around.

Within a year Roger and the other members of The Who were all millionaires – a remarkable transformation in their finances. 'Until *Tommy* we were flat broke and busted,' Roger admitted. He estimated that before *Tommy* The Who were around two million dollars in debt. Now the album was a runaway success, and the band that once wrecked their instruments to get noticed at small, dingy clubs were on course to appear, thanks to Kit Lambert's imaginative bookings, in opera houses around the world.

No longer was there any need to end their shows with an orgy of delinquent destruction. This in turn meant huge and very welcome savings on repairs and new equipment, although not everyone in the band was totally satisfied at The Who being elevated by *Tommy* to the darlings of the international jet set. 'We turned into snob rock,' said John Entwistle. 'We were the kind of band Jackie Onassis would come and see, and I didn't particularly like that. I felt we should have played opera houses and smashed them up.'

Crucially for Roger, he had at last found his voice within The Who through the songs Townshend wrote for the rock opera. 'In *Tommy*, it was to do with being an actor and finding the character,' he says. 'It gave me the chance to explore and develop all those sides of me to make the stories live in a dramatic sense.' But there was a down side. As vocal narrator of *Tommy*, Roger came to embody *Tommy*, especially after film director Ken Russell turned the rock opera into a movie.

Roger recalls: 'Pete used to write his best stuff when he was writing about a character that he could see very, very clearly from outside himself, when he is writing about a figure beyond himself. And I was that figure. And of course I personified Tommy. I was the guy who used to play the part. I played the damn part for five years. I slogged my balls off around the world sweating it out.

People thought I was Tommy. I used to get called Tommy in the street.'

From the earliest performances of *Tommy*, Roger could sense that The Who had been elevated to an altogether different plane in the rock hierarchy. Instead of playing a string of three-minute pop songs, the group were now presenting elongated pieces which amounted to a flowing performance of almost an hour and a half. The rock opera had given them a chance to stretch themselves, and audiences were now sitting back and listening and applauding at the end. Roger, as the on-stage personification of Tommy, was accorded a standing ovation every night.

Roger noticed too that within the band there appeared to be a new camaraderie. Certainly Pete was treating him with new-found respect. '*Tommy* was huge,' Pete says. 'It made Roger into a proper frontman. He was magnificent on stage from this time forwards. I felt as if a huge weight had been lifted. I think I probably resented that there was yet another glamour boy on stage (apart from Keith and his goo-goo eyes) but the pros outweighed the cons. The women backstage were prettier. And Roger was almost always very, very happy.'

Pete, being Pete, admits he nevertheless didn't fully appreciate just how good Roger was until some three years later, in 1973, when American producer Lou Reizner staged *Tommy* at the Rainbow Theatre in Finsbury Park, north London. On this occasion Pete was not part of the production but a member of the audience. It was the first time he had ever seen Roger from the stalls rather than as a fellow performer on stage. He was astounded.

'He was great,' Pete told *Uncut* magazine. 'I'd always thought Roger was a bit naff, I'd always thought he was a bit of a nuisance – y'know, swinging his microphone and getting in the way of my guitar sound. That was the moment I realised that, through *Tommy*, Roger had made this connection to the audience and become a theatrical performer. I had much greater respect for him after that.

'*Tommy* made Roger a singer, it made Roger an icon, it made Roger like Jim Morrison [of the Doors] or like Robert Plant [of Led Zeppelin] or, like, the Lead Singer. It gave him the right to grow his hair and wear the tassel jacket and swing his mike around instead of just posing and looking angry and, like, "Don't fuck with me," which isn't who he is by any means, but it gave him a vehicle, it gave him a part that he could play.'

While the success of *Tommy* at last gave Roger the vocal identity within The Who's music that he had long been seeking, the ensuing fortunes from massive record sales, stage presentation rights and performances also meant he could finally look for the home of his dreams.

The years he had spent with Heather in the Berkshire countryside had given him a taste for rural living and old houses, and he came to recognise that his days as even a part-time Londoner were over. This view was strengthened when The Who returned in mid-August 1971 from another gruelling tour of America and were quickly booked to headline a charity concert in aid of the Bangladesh Relief Fund at the Oval cricket ground in south London on 18 September 1971.

A crowd of 31,000 gave the band a rapturous reception and the event raised £18,336, with The Who donating 25% of the gross box-office takings to the relief fund. The event was a resounding success, but for Roger it was also a turning point in his life. He enjoyed festivals, and this one at the Oval was no exception, but he couldn't help but notice how foul London's air seemed, how frantic the pace of the capital and how the car took precedence over people. It was the same in most cities, of course, but he had always loved London and now he simply felt that the capital was no longer a place where he could live.

'I'd just come back from [touring] America and I hadn't realised how much like America London had become,' he said. 'It was awful, smelled awful, and yet I used to love London. I looked around and thought that the quality of life in the city was nothing.

The people there just didn't seem to realise it. I found it very sad. I wanted to breathe fresh air every day.'

Roger's solution was to purchase Holmhurst Manor, a magnificent rambling Jacobean mansion set in 35 acres of rolling countryside at Burwash in East Sussex, near the border with Kent. Roger paid just under the asking price of £39,000, and admitted: 'I didn't have the money to buy it. I was just sort of looking at houses because I love old buildings, but when I saw this one I knew I had to live here.'

Several of Roger's associates were quick to tell him he was making a big mistake buying an old place in the middle of the country and one that needed considerable and probably costly refurbishment. They warned him too that he might find it very difficult to sell the property again at some future date, but Roger's mind was made up. He was enthralled by the majestic high walls, the stained-glass windows created by the Pre-Raphaelite artist Burne-Jones, the atmosphere engendered by the house's history. Its solid foundations and seclusion met his own need for a solid base and privacy. He also saw it as the perfect place for himself and Heather to bring up the family they wanted to have. 'I bought it because I needed it,' he protested, 'and it needed me. Sounds silly, but that's how it was.'

Ironworking was a highly profitable industry in East Sussex in the seventeenth century, and Holmhurst Manor had been built in 1610 by one of the Sussex ironmasters and there had once been a foundry on the premises. The 35 acres that came with Roger's new home contained a swimming pool, two lakes, a cottage, garaging, stabling and other outbuildings. The house was not far from Bateman's, another characteristically Jacobean mansion built by a wealthy ironmaster, which was the home of Rudyard Kipling for 34 years until his death in 1936. It was there, surrounded by his library, that he wrote many of his books, including *Puck of Pook's Hill*.

Once he had moved in, Roger didn't go up to London for two

whole months. He just revelled in his new surroundings and relished finding a new life in a setting steeped in history. From the house he was able to gaze out over neat lawns, admire the rhododendrons and catch sight of pheasants flying over golden fields. 'I'd never live in London again,' he told visitors as he strolled happily around his estate in his wellies. But it irked him if attempts were made in subsequent interviews to portray him as Squire Daltrey, lord of the manor, the former Shepherd's Bush tough guy gone all posh. 'I didn't get the house as a status symbol,' he insisted. 'I really didn't. I'm not into that rubbish about a pop star with a big house.'

Nevertheless, the six-bedroomed house, with its fabulous stone fireplaces and wooden balcony with inlaid religious carvings, could not help but lend itself to touches of grandeur. The oak-panelled library was filled with much-treasured leather-bound books, and Roger decorated the master bedroom in restful pale gold and installed an imposing four-poster bed standing on a peach-coloured carpet. Above the bed, staring down from the ceiling, were clusters of ornate cherubs.

But it was the tranquillity and simplicity of country life that really appealed to Roger after the hustle and bustle of the cities he visited on tour with The Who. After countless mad rushes from stage to limousine to the temporary sanctuary of yet another hotel room, he had had enough of city life. 'I'm happy just pruning a garden,' he said. 'I'd rather live in a tent than live up in London again. If I wasn't a musician I think I'd be happy as a farm labourer earning £20 to £30 a week rather than earning two or three times that in a factory. I always said that if ever I made any money, this was how I'd live – and I've done it.'

While other rich rock stars surrounded themselves with servants and staff at the country piles they acquired courtesy of their royalties, Roger employed just one man to help him with the land. He preferred to roll up his sleeves and work on his property himself. He toiled away on the roof, set about much of the interior redecorating and even dug out his trout lake with his own personal bulldozer, a giant yellow toy which gave him great pleasure when he jumped into the driver's seat and began playing with the controls.

The sheer hard physical work, he soon came to realise, was the perfect antidote to the madness that surrounded The Who on the road. He liked to get his hands dirty, bricklaying, lugging heavy bags of cement or spending three days personally laying down the gravel drive which led up to the house from the wrought-iron entry gates.

During great bursts of activity, weary old hedges were swept away to open up far-reaching views across woods and fields rolling away almost to the coast. Eventually the grounds included a great waterfall and a rock garden, an old tennis court became a swimming pool and Roger created a temple-like gazebo from pillars he discovered in the Old Kent Road which stood sentinel-like at the start of a woodland path.

A cat and three dogs soon took up residence and Roger also tried his hand at farming, acquiring 45 Friesian cows. Later he added a further 280 acres to his property by buying up two neighbouring farms and the 200 head of cattle that went with them. 'Our lives are very unglamorous,' said Roger after he and Heather had settled in. 'We never go out to clubs or trendy parties. I think Ashford cattle market is much more entertaining.'

The arrival of two daughters in quick succession, Rosie Lea (cockney rhyming slang for tea) and Willow, followed five years later by a son, Jamie, provided the young brood that Roger and Heather desperately wanted and which the big old house needed to fulfil its family potential. When the children were old enough to enjoy the heated outdoor swimming pool, Roger issued an open invitation to children from the village to come and enjoy splashing around in it as well. And for fun, he would take himself off to his timbered workshop to spend a day repairing old fairground carousels and gypsy caravans, or painstakingly make beautiful doll's houses, complete with red roofs, for Rosie and Willow.

In keeping with country living and the work he was putting into his home, Roger adopted a healthy regime of getting up at eight, eating a hearty breakfast and then working right through the day without eating again until he sat down for supper at seven or eight in the evening.

Friends who visited Roger at the new house had never seen him happier. His harmonious domesticity with Heather and the children was much envied by other, less stable rock stars. 'Heather has proved to be the most incredibly supportive wife to Roger and as a mother bringing up their kids,' observes Keith Altham, The Who's former publicist and a good friend of Roger's. 'I don't think Roger could have had a better wife. She's the best thing that has happened to him. She has always been a very level-headed woman – she has lots of common sense and a wonderfully objective attitude towards the business.

'She sees the nonsense around rock 'n' roll, and she sees the realistic aspects, and she doesn't have any illusions about it. She doesn't distance herself from the business completely, but she certainly made her family her priority and she's one of the most sensible people I know in ordinary life. She managed to keep a family and a lovely family home for Roger to go back to after the circus that was The Who, after the madness surrounding rock 'n' roll, and help him feel normal again and a reasonable human being.

'It's a very insane business, and you wonder how some people are still alive after all the pressure and the tension, drugs and drink. If you don't have some kind of normality to go back to, then you don't survive. Heather has provided that, and Roger's survived.

'Roger stayed away from all the drugs. He'd have a drink, but I think he knew the drugs would mess him up and his voice. He also knew what he did on stage was quite physically demanding and if he got into all that he knew he wouldn't be able to do it. He always had a natural sense of survival and what you needed to do to get through it. He very quickly saw the dangers of over-indulgence. Roger was always an anchor in that respect.'

CHAPTER NINE

LIVE AND KICKING

Roger is one of the few people who can and will take him [Pete Townshend] on, usually with monumental frustration and sometimes justifiable anger, I think, that he's being dismissed in some way or another.

Keith Altham

How to follow *Tommy* was always going to prove a headache for The Who, particularly for its composer, Pete Townshend. After spectacularly pulling off their attempt at artful glory with *Tommy*, Roger was keen for the band now to reassert itself as a rock force. The problem was partially, but only temporarily, solved by the band starting the new decade by taking the Pye mobile studio up to Leeds to record an album intended to capture the excitement of their live performances.

Recorded at Leeds University refectory on 14 February 1970, *Live at Leeds* set a standard for in-concert albums which countless groups and singers have tried to match ever since. Very few have succeeded.

While *Tommy* was sophisticated, highbrow rock opera, *Live at Leeds* was The Who back to the raw power that had always been their calling card. When released in May 1970, the LP was even covered crudely in clicking noises, which, according to Pete, were caused by a 'dodgy mike cable'. This prompted the inclusion of a note on the circular label of the album that read: 'Crackling noises OK. Do not correct.' As well as a version of 'My Generation' consisting of a jam lasting almost 15 minutes, the album included majestically noisy, heavy-rock covers of Mose Allison's 'Young Man Blues', Eddie Cochran's 'C'mon Everybody' and Johnny Kidd and the Pirates' 'Shakin' All Over'.

'I've always maintained they were the greatest rock 'n' roll band because they were north, south, east and west,' says Keith Altham. 'Each was diametrically opposed to each other and when they got together they put together something that was quite beautiful. It's almost like Gestalt, the German word, a unique blend which presented something they couldn't and have never been able to do individually. Collectively there was an extraordinary balance of four people coming together and finding a perfect harmony. On some nights when they played, without any of them being brilliantly individual musicians – not an Eric Clapton or a Jeff Beck or a Rod Stewart or a Michael Hutchence, in other words without a superstar in there – they did something that I've never seen equalled. I've seen all the bands, all the supergroups, but I've never seen a band with that kind of blend that could provide that unique unity. *Live at Leeds* best captures that on record.'

Live at Leeds kept Who fans happy enough. But it brought to a close the most prolific phase of the group's recording career. In the seventies they released only four albums of new material and in the eighties just three. During periods of inactivity by the band, Roger contented himself with working on his farm, expanding his forays into acting, and generally enjoying his home in Sussex.

Roger had worked hard to convert one of the barns on his land into a well-equipped recording studio. Soon he struck up a friendship with Adam Faith, who also lived in Sussex and was managing the young singer-songwriter Leo Sayer. Roger was introduced to Adam by Keith Altham, who had known the sixties pop star for many years. Altham recalled: 'I said: "Adam, you're in Brighton, Leo's in Brighton, Roger's in Sussex just down the road. So why don't you all get together and maybe you can come to some sort of deal about using Roger's recording studio?" They got on like a house on fire. That led directly to Roger making a solo album with a lot of Leo Sayer compositions.'

The album, *Daltrey*, was recorded at Roger's studio and surprised many with a feel that was much gentler than his work with The Who. In the spring of 1973 a single taken from it, 'Giving It All Away', reached number five in the charts. Roger was suitably serious when choosing and recording different kinds of material for his solo releases, but he nevertheless tended to regard his status as a solo singer as a hobby or diversion from his main job as The Who's frontman. Although he would make further solo albums at intervals, he has gone on record to state that *Daltrey* is the only one that he is now happy to stand by. Speaking to *Q* magazine, he even went so far as to describe his 1977 LP *One of the Boys* as 'a poxy, complete piece-of-crap album'.

The second solo album, *Ride a Rock Horse*, which came out in June 1975, was mediocre. It was notable mainly for its striking cover picture of Roger as a centaur, half man half horse, for his version of Phillip Goodhand-Tait's ballad 'Oceans Away', sung with soaring clarity, and for tackling the Rufus Thomas chestnut 'Walking the Dog' in his own way.

Roger's main motive in asserting his independence was to try out his voice on songs written by songwriters other than Pete Townshend. But he was not surprised to find that for songs of weight and relevance, songs that suited his own voice and interpretation, his bandmate had no equal. It didn't, however, stop promoters offering Roger stupendous amounts of money to take on a solo tour, which he nevertheless declined.

One such carrot, back in 1977, was $500,000 for Roger to do two shows at Madison Square Garden in New York. With typical logic, Roger decided that this would not only take up too much energy, but would also elevate his ego too high for his own good. The important thing about The Who, he reasoned, was for each member of the band to keep his ego at a level that allowed the group to survive. An over-inflated sense of self, he felt, could damage The Who, and he was not prepared to risk it himself.

The lucrative offer came on the back of his third solo album, the self-maligned *One of the Boys*, which forsook ballads for rock with the help of a clutch of established songwriters such as Steve Gibbons, Paul McCartney, Phillip Goodhand-Tait, Colin Blunstone and Murray Head. Roger also contributed three of the songs himself, including 'The Prisoner', which was inspired by his meeting with John McVicar, a reformed villain whose life Roger was soon to portray on film.

Fifteen months after the rapturous reception of *Live at Leeds*, August 1971 saw the release of *Who's Next*, regarded by many as the band's finest album, with Roger at his most vocally assured. For 'Won't Get Fooled Again', a tough song of disillusionment which was recently voted by Who fans as the band's greatest song, Roger summoned up an extraordinary blood-curdling scream mid-song. For 'Behind Blue Eyes', a Townshend composition written about Roger and his restrained anger, the singer showed he could handle a powerful ballad backed by acoustic guitars as well as anyone.

Who's Next contained remnants of Pete Townshend's abandoned *Lifehouse* project, which was about a near-future world where people were controlled by a compulsory link to a national grid. Townshend had intended *Lifehouse* to be a grand-scale follow-up to *Tommy*, but the idea was so convoluted that he could not get it over clearly to those he needed to understand it most.

'Pete has these wonderful ideas that balloon out of all comprehension,' says Keith Altham. 'And Roger would say: "Yes, Pete, it might be a good idea to rule the universe, but let's start with Shepherd's Bush." The *Lifehouse* project was one that never really got together because Roger couldn't see it. And neither could I, and I was doing the PR for it.

'I could see Pete had a clever idea there, an interesting concept, the idea of a grid going into people's homes and people living vicariously through other people's lives – reality TV is not too far away from it. But I couldn't see where Pete's *Lifehouse* was going to go. Interestingly it later transpired as the Internet – Pete's very clever at seeing ways in which things might be likely to develop in the future. He's quite prophetic in some ways. And he's also very good at encompassing the feeling of the time, like *Quadrophenia*. Sometimes that's easier to cope with than some of his more inflated over-intellectualisations of concepts. But Roger's the guy who would say: "It's great, but it won't work unless we've got this and do that." And of course that drew him into conflict with Pete.

'No hugely creative person wants to hear his sunflowers might not work if they are not painted in a particular way. But Pete needs the conflict and confrontation, and Roger is one of the few people who can and will take him on, usually with monumental frustration and sometimes justifiable anger, I think, that he's being dismissed in some way or another.

'And Pete to his credit will look at it and say: "Well actually, I hadn't thought of it that way. You might actually be right." Pete desperately needs people to sound off, to bounce ideas off, which was where Kit Lambert was so important in the beginning and he's never quite had that same person since. He's never had an intellectual equal that could kind of compete with him in that way.

'Pete has a tendency to over-think, and Roger at one point had a tendency to under-think. But now he's balanced that out and he's got something to offer, more than Pete realises or Pete is prepared to admit. There have been fractures in the relationship – just like a marriage, major rows and walk-outs. Pete is such a forceful arguer that he can convince himself he is right when it's something that is not necessarily correct. He's such a good arguer that he almost convinces himself he's right. It takes somebody to suddenly come in and say: "Well actually, no, you're not right", because he bullies his way through something, quite enjoys bullying his way through, and knows he's bullying in a strange way. Not physically, but cerebrally. Unless someone like Roger stands up to him, ideas get lost. If it hadn't been for Roger, a lot of things The Who achieved would never have taken place.

'Sometimes Roger needs confronting too. He can be very obstinate. He can be moved if the argument is sufficiently strong and convincing – and if you're prepared to take him on. Because if you're not, then he won't be convinced that the argument is worthwhile. When he turns those laser-blue eyes on you and you've got his full attention, if you haven't got a good argument or an explanation, then God help you!

'As a singer Roger is quite aware of his own limitations. He's someone who has matured a great deal since the early 1960s, he's learned and absorbed extra knowledge both in terms of production in the studio and how to write songs, but he doesn't pretend that he had the genius Pete had to write songs. But he's worked solo and is capable of doing so – he's had solo albums, worked in movies and TV series and he's been able to prove to himself that he's not without talent when he's without Townshend.

'Maybe that was a problem for him at one stage, but it would have been for anyone up against Pete, who was so all-productive and all-consuming, all-absorbing, that it was very difficult for anyone else to get a look in or to compete with him as he was so talented. Roger couldn't compete but he could hold his own ground – which was what Roger was good at. He's a great adapter and a great survivor. He can adapt and can learn.

'In the early days he was the kind of guy who would settle an argument with fists and a right hook, but he realised there were better ways of going about it otherwise you run out of friends rather quickly or people to work with. He didn't learn much at school but learned – that great cliché – everything from the school of life. But he has learned, he's a much more balanced, rounded individual. I have a lot of admiration for him 'cos of his common sense and his pragmatism.'

Roger and Keith Altham were not the only ones who found the *Lifehouse* concept impossible to grasp. Despite his best efforts Pete could fully convince only a few of the full validity of *Lifehouse*. But the subsequent abandonment of the project was The Who's gain when it came to recording *Who's Next*. 'Won't Get Fooled Again', 'Baba O'Riley', 'Bargain' and 'Behind Blue Eyes', once destined for *Lifehouse*, emerged as among Pete's finest songs.

Within two years Pete had completed another Who concept, *Quadrophenia*, an album of songs about the life and frustration of a young sixties Mod called Jimmy. A much more complex project than *Tommy*, *Quadrophenia*, released in October 1973, combined a nostalgic look back at an era when The Who were in their element with a psychological exploration of the four 'quadrophonic' sides of Jimmy's character. Each Who member would embody one aspect: Roger as the toughie, Keith as the lunatic, Pete as the hypocrite and John as the romantic. As with *Tommy*, Pete's concept was extended into a movie, and this launched the acting careers of Leslie Ash, Phil Daniels as the pill-popping fashion-mad Mod and Sting as the weekend super-Mod whose image collapses when it's revealed he works as a bellboy.

It was while the band were rehearsing '5.15', one of the more memorable *Quadrophenia* songs to come Roger's way, that the most violent of confrontations occurred between him and Pete. A film crew were filming the rehearsal and Roger became miffed that they still appeared to be sitting on their equipment cases idling the time away without a camera turning while he sang through most of *Quadrophenia*. Indignantly, he turned on them and asked if they were going to wait until he had worn his voice out before they deigned to start filming. *Quadrophenia* was tough to sing, he explained, and he was not going to sing it twice for their benefit.

According to Roger, Pete then came over to him and started poking him in the chest and telling him to do as he was told. As the situation appeared to be turning ugly, roadies jumped in and held Roger down and Pete then hit Roger across the shoulder with his

Gibson guitar. Roger's version is that Pete then spat and swore at him and demanded the roadies let Roger go so he could lay into him.

'So they let me go,' Roger recalled, 'and he threw two punches. One went to the side of my head and he threw the other and it goes on the other side. And he was throwing a right at me and he was totally off balance, so I hit him with an upper cut and he went six inches off the ground and passed out. And I had to escort him to hospital because I thought I had killed him. No one was sorrier than I. But it wasn't a big fight. He was pissed and he thought he could fight me and he can't fight me. I mean, you have to know how to fight.'

Later Roger played down the incident when he told the *New Musical Express*: 'It was a bit of a non-argument. The last thing in the world I wanted to do was have a fist fight with Pete Townshend. Unfortunately he hit me first with a guitar. I really felt terrible about it afterwards. What can you say? Pete should never try and be a fighter, but when he's being held back by two roadies and he's spitting at me, calling me a dirty little c*** and hitting me with his guitar, I became quite angry. I was forced to lay one on him. But it was only one.'

As luck would have it, the managing director from The Who's American record company had chosen that day to watch The Who rehearsing and had been promised he would be able to meet the members of the band personally. It was Keith Altham, as The Who's PR, who was entrusted with escorting the MD to the sound stage and the two of them arrived just at the moment Roger threw the immaculate right hook which laid Pete flat out. Altham remembers Roger instantly being filled with remorse and dropping to his knees, cradling head's Pete in his arms, telling him he loved him and calling for an ambulance.

'Holy shit!' was the MD's horrified reaction to this unexpected punch-up while waiting excitedly to be introduced to the band. 'Are they always like this?' he enquired nervously of Altham. 'No,' replied Keith, 'today is one of their better days – shall we repair to the bar until all the judges' votes have been counted?'

Roger resorting to fisticuffs may have been a rare lapse in his guise of Peaceful Perce, but there was no disguising the fact that he and Pete were at loggerheads as much as ever. In the spring of 1975 Pete infuriated Roger by giving an interview in the music press in which he talked about the dangers of The Who turning into a golden-oldies act and the unappetising prospect of the band 'rocking in our wheelchairs'.

Townshend told the journalist: 'When we were gigging in this country in the early part of last year, I was thoroughly depressed. I honestly felt that The Who were going on stage every night and, for the sake of die-hard fans, copying what The Who used to be.' Roger's response was: 'I never read such a load of bullshit in my life.'

By the time the next LP, *The Who by Numbers*, was released, in October of that year, the songs were reflecting Pete Townshend's midlife crisis. 'However Much I Booze' was Pete laying bare his dependence on alcohol and was such a personal song that Roger refused to sing it. Extracted as a single, 'Squeeze Box' managed to make the Top Ten in the UK and number 16 in America. The album was well received, reaching number seven in the UK LP charts and number eight in the States.

CHAPTER TEN

ACTING

I'd had no acting training. I was even turned down for the
school play – so the fact that Tommy was deaf, dumb and
blind was a Godsend.

Roger Daltrey

For Roger, it all began again with *Tommy*. Life as a semi-retired
rock star with a string of business interests was never going to be
anything like enough to satisfy The Who's human dynamo. He
needed a new passion and a new area to target with his boundless
energy and enthusiasm. And with the film version of *Tommy* he
found acting, and a whole new career.

The creation of *Tommy* was a good example of the remarkable
synergy between members of The Who and their management.
Pete Townshend's fertile imagination carefully carved out the final
details of the rock opera in 1969, but the concept had been around
for much longer than that. Roger Daltrey's memory is that the idea
for *Tommy* actually began with the charismatic Kit Lambert.

A man full of innovations, Kit had it in his head that The
Who should do a rock opera on a grand scale, demonstrating
their talents to different audiences. He was passionate in his
belief that rock deserved its rightful place in the musical world

and all his life fought against rock being belittled or downtrodden simply because it was popular and emotive. Kit's intellect and his background as the son of a classical composer meant he was 'from the other side', as the band used to describe it. He was proud of rock 'n' roll, and he was totally committed to achieving its acceptance as an art form, but he was well aware of all the other areas of music. And he was determined to deliver The Who to as wide a following as possible, crossing boundaries between different kinds of music whenever he could. And one of the ways to break those barriers, Kit said when the idea was still unheard of, was to do a rock opera.

So Pete came up with a song called 'Amazing Journey,' about a guy going through life deaf, dumb and blind. All his experiences were through his sense of touch. *Tommy* grew from that song. But most of the pushing was done by Kit. He had a hell of a lot to do with it, insists Roger. The striking theme of the story was at least partly inspired by Townshend's difficult and unhappy childhood in the immediate post-war years. The guitarist's early years were deeply marred by his parents' desperately unhappy marriage. The 'deaf, dumb and blind kid' Tommy typified a child totally traumatised by his early experiences.

It has been said that the idea of *Tommy* was at least partly sparked by the Sonny Boy Williamson song 'Eyesight to the Blind'. Townshend, not one for lengthy explanations of his thought processes, would much rather play music than analyse its sources of inspiration. However, *Tommy* was a very personal creation of his, and years later he did venture: 'I was trying to show that even though we had not been in the war we suffered its echo.'

Tommy was a huge success on record and later on stage. It won five Tonys, a Grammy and an Olivier. Producer Robert Stigwood was full of enthusiasm for the potential of a film version. Negotiations were difficult and protracted, but by 1973 they were more or less complete and Stigwood put the cat among the artistic pigeons by signing brilliant but controversial director Ken Russell to bring Townshend's vibrant vision to the screen.

Roger had sung the part of Tommy on stage for years and naturally took the role in the film, although he admitted to friends at the time that, while he was certainly enthusiastic about becoming a film star, he 'hadn't got the remotest clue of what to expect'. Later he noted dryly that if he had known what to expect he would have been unable to believe it.

'I'd had no acting training,' he said. 'I was even turned down for the school play – so the fact that Tommy was deaf, dumb and blind was a godsend.' And he was only half joking. He was certainly up for a new challenge, but he also realised that he was moving into a totally new area of performance, playing a key central role which carried great responsibility for the success of the whole enterprise. The other members of The Who were heavily involved, but only Keith Moon had an acting part, as Tommy's deeply suspect Uncle Ernie.

Stigwood used his considerable pull and influence in Hollywood to persuade the popular and successful American actress Ann-Margret to take on the pivotal role of Tommy's mother. Remarkably, the producer also managed to secure cameo appearances by Tina Turner and Jack Nicholson.

The film was massively changed from Pete Townshend's original stage version. Ken Russell arrived with a single casting demand, that the part of Tommy's Uncle Frank should go to his favourite star, the controversial and consistently outrageous Oliver Reed. This presented an instant problem as all the dialogue in *Tommy* was to be delivered in song. Although Reed was an immensely talented actor, he freely admitted that he couldn't sing a note. And, to make matters worse, he found even miming to songs desperately difficult. But Russell had enormous faith in Reed's ability to add colour and life to the film and insisted anyone could be tutored to sing adequately. But Reed's first attempts at song didn't impress Pete Townshend or Roger Daltrey and they began to wonder if the controversial director was right to foist this self-confessed hellraiser on the production.

But one man didn't care a jot that Oliver Reed was no singer. Keith Moon recognised other, much more interesting talents in the big man from the movies who liked to live life in the fast lane. More specifically, he saw a colourful kindred spirit who approached life with as much alcoholic assistance as he could manage and simply refused to take anything seriously. It was the start of a great friendship, packed with hilariously outrageous incidents, that continued until Moon's untimely early death.

Roger told friends at the time that the similarity between the two wild men of the entertainment business was remarkable, not to say frightening. They were both very unusual, fabulously talented guys, he said, and individually they were often not easy to handle. But together they were frequently impossible. One day on location Moon was disturbed to discover that he had left his favourite jacket in Roger's hotel room. No one could instantly find a key, so Moon borrowed a large electric drill from one of the film crew and proceeded to hammer-drill his way inside. 'Roger was furious when he found out what had happened,' said Reed later, 'particularly as Keith spent some time in the room with a couple of rather attractive lady friends. The room was a complete shambles afterwards.'

Ken Russell also found Moon difficult at times, but all the members of The Who generally threw themselves into the project with an enthusiasm which impressed the director. 'I was told before I started the film that I was mad to be associated with rock stars,' said Russell. 'They were notorious for unpunctuality, not turning up, blowing up toilets … all true, I'm sure. But maybe it was because it was Pete Townshend's dream child, everyone rallied around him to do the very best they could. I didn't have to direct Roger Daltrey, because he'd been associated with it for so long that he was faultless.'

In January 1974 all the performers polished their singing talents before meeting in the studio in February to record the film's musical tracks. Ann-Margret, who confessed later she had never heard of Roger Daltrey, *Tommy* or even The Who, had nonetheless diligently learned all of her 11 songs in advance and had even spent the flight across the Atlantic from her home in the United States perfecting them. Roger was impressed with such professionalism and he was also impressed by Miss Margret's sex appeal, even if she was there to play his mother. The Who were generally cool about show-business rivals but the Hollywood charisma of the beautiful actress went down exceptionally well. And it proved a huge contrast to the clowning and lunacy brought to the set by the combination of Oliver Reed and Keith Moon.

Ken Russell was not perturbed by Oliver Reed's musical shortcomings. In fact, he had such confidence in the actor that he proceeded to drastically alter Kit Lambert's original script in such a way as to exchange Moon's large role with Reed's much smaller part. Oliver Reed plays a large part in the film as Tommy's villainous 'uncle', Frank, who kills the boy's father after being discovered in bed with his mother. Originally Moon's character Uncle Ernie performed this dramatic function, but in the finished version Ernie was reduced to little more than Frank's stooge. Roger recalls that Moon was something of a handful on the production. The unpredictable drummer arrived some six hours late for one session and it was left to his new friend Oliver Reed to speak up to prevent Russell from reducing Moon's role even further. 'If Ken had had his way, Keith wouldn't have been involved at all,' said Reed.

Tommy's story is told almost entirely in music. Apart from a few exceptional lines all the words delivered by the characters are sung. The action begins towards the end of the Second World War with some tender scenes between a young married couple who are very much in love. Robert Powell plays dashing RAF bomber pilot Group Captain Walker, while Ann-Margret plays his wife, Nora. We first see them spending a blissful holiday together while Walker is on leave. They swim naked in mountain pools and then make love passionately in a forest glade. It seems an idyllic relationship, but their happiness is shattered when the horror of war intrudes. With echoes of Roger's own extraordinary birth, an air raid strikes London with frightening ferocity and the couple are shocked to find the dead body of a child in a wrecked house. But, his leave over, Walker bids Nora a tearful farewell at a railway station.

Nora is mortified when she receives the terrible news of her husband's loss – his aeroplane is shot down over Germany – while she is at work packing ball bearings in a grim munitions factory. But, unknown to either of them, Walker has left his wife pregnant and a few months later, on 8 May 1945, VE (Victory in Europe) Day, Nora gives birth to their son, whom she names Tommy. 'It's a boy,' sing the medical staff as the celebrations go on wildly outside. Nora and her young son, played by gifted child actor Barry Winch, join other grieving widows to plant a cross with a poppy to remember her brave husband.

Life has to go on, and Nora takes Tommy, who is now six years old, to stay at Bernie's Holiday Camp, where she meets the handsome and instantly attentive 'greencoat' host Frank Hobbs, played by Oliver Reed at his most saturnine. 'Call me Uncle Frank,' sings Reed in his own inimitable style from underneath a colossal quiff. He can scarcely contain his lust as Nora wins a Miss Lovely Legs contest. The mutual attraction is overwhelming and Nora and Frank quickly become lovers and decide to marry and live together in her house with young Tommy, who idolises his dashing 'uncle'.

But, of course, no one is going to be allowed to live happily ever after and it turns out that Group Captain Walker survived his horrific plane crash after all and, out of the blue and very inconveniently, he turns up, horribly scarred. In the flurry of exotic images, it is not explained exactly why Walker has taken six years to return home, but naturally the war hero is outraged when he finds his loving bride in bed with Frank. A colourful fight ensues, which is won by Frank – Oliver Reed here is at his most muscular – who smashes the life out of his rival with a heavy bedside lamp. Tommy witnesses this shocking violence and is totally traumatised, becoming the 'deaf, dumb and blind boy' who is at the centre of the story.

Poor Tommy is instantly plunged into a terrifying dark secret world of his own. Nora and Frank try in vain to stimulate the lad, Frank soon losing patience and frequently becoming furiously frustrated. They take Tommy to a funfair and hold an extravagant Christmas party, but he remains hopelessly trapped in his black, silent world. Years go by and Tommy, now played by an eerily blank-looking Roger Daltrey, has grown into a young man. In desperation Nora and Frank take Tommy to a bizarre faith-healing preacher, played by a somewhat vague-looking Eric Clapton, who worships enormous images of Marilyn Monroe. Ken Russell's famous enthusiasm for challenging established religious beliefs came into play in the scenes of the handicapped queuing up in their wheelchairs (including one containing the director in a brief appearance) to pay homage to a statue of Marilyn with her dress blowing skywards. This does not seem to help Tommy at all.

He is then taken to the scary, self-styled 'Acid Queen', played by Tina Turner, who enables Tommy to see a weird red image of himself thanks to the injection of thousands of shots of drugs. But Tommy's life hardly improves when Nora and Frank leave him for a time with Cousin Kevin, played by Paul Nicholas, who turns out to be a sadistic bully who cruelly mistreats him. At one point the poor chap is even strapped to an ironing board and pressed. And his life gets worse when the perverted Uncle Ernie (Keith Moon) is left in charge of the still handicapped Tommy while Nora and Frank go out for the evening. Ernie takes Tommy to bed and the experience is so shattering for the young man that he is stunned into regaining more of his visual powers.

Tommy walks from the room into a strange scrapyard, where he finds a spectacular pinball machine which, miraculously, he starts to play brilliantly. His score reaches one billion and the crowd which has witnessed his skill goes wild and hails him as the new champion of the world. The previous supremo, played by Elton

John, delivers the memorable song 'Pinball Wizard' in tribute. Suddenly Tommy has gone from virtual vegetable to international superstar and Frank is quick to cash in on the fame. Nora feels guilty as Tommy is still severely handicapped, and she has a terrible nervous breakdown. She sings her devastating lament alone in her luxury hotel room in a stunning scene which climaxes when she hurls a champagne bottle through the television set. The TV then spews out foam, followed by several lorryloads of baked beans for her to writhe about in suggestively. It is perhaps the most memorable section of the film and is said to be a blast against commercialism, but interpretations vary wildly about what on earth it means.

Frank hears of a new specialist who might cure Tommy, but the medic, played by Jack Nicholson, can't help, for all the alarming innuendo he conveys with his eyebrows. Back at home, Nora is driven to distraction by the sight of Tommy gazing endlessly at his image in the mirror and furiously hurls him into the glass. There is a shattering explosion and what seems like a miracle as Tommy is released at last from his dark and lonely prison. Suddenly he regains his hearing, speech and sight, and flies around with joy, cartwheeling across beaches and hurtling apparently round the globe with elation at his release. So happy is he with his transformation that he is convinced he is the new Messiah. He holds huge religious gatherings so that he can bless the faithful in person. Pretty teenager Sally, played by the director's daughter, Victoria Russell, is desperate to touch her idol. The crush is intense, but she bravely battles to the edge of the stage, where she is cruelly booted to the floor by Frank and badly injured in the process.

Special Tommy Holiday Camps spring up all over the world in the astonishing spiritual rebirth inspired by Tommy's story. Eventually, however, Tommy's devoted followers become tired of their leader and smash pinball machines at the camps in an angry and destructive rebellion. In the onslaught, Nora and Frank are violently killed. But Tommy is freed by this rejection and as the story ends he is full of life and hope, and experiences a sense of total rebirth, in the wild terrain where he was conceived. The film is an extraordinary piece of work that has surely inspired countless pop videos, many nowhere near as imaginative.

For any actor, playing the title role in this weird and wonderful musical movie would have been a challenge. For a pop star completely untrained in the dramatic arts it was a mind-blowing experience. But Roger wisely placed confidence in his charismatic director and it was a decision he never regretted. 'I think it takes film into a new dimension,' he said. 'The way Ken has cut the scenes together is like a record there are so many facets to it. Before we started working on the film I did not realise just how difficult it was going to be. I didn't have anything to act with. I felt like a vegetable most of the time. I tried to do it inwardly and somehow or other I seem to have got my soul on that film. It was very heavy. Some days I was "blind", some days I was not; that was very difficult and very weird. The first day I could actually do anything normal, I felt like a blind man getting his sight back.'

When shooting began, in April, the female lead was still rather confused about her role. 'I spent the first few days of production trailing Pete Townshend asking him questions about my character,' said Ann-Margret in her autobiography, *My Story*. 'Since I had never done a film remotely like *Tommy*, which was as wild and exaggerated as a hallucination, I wrote reams of notes and studied them before each scene.' Despite her continuing confusion, she found director Ken Russell 'wild, indulgent, kind and funny'.

But no one was laughing when Ann-Margret became the first casualty by gashing her hand in the scene where she smashes the television screen with the champagne bottle. The painful wound needed 27 stitches, but, bravely, she was back on set the next day, hiding her bandaged hand under a table during filming.

Keith Moon fell head over heels in love with Ann-Margret long before the movie was completed, charmingly describing her to anyone who would listen as 'a lovely girl with big tits'. When she innocently admired a large diamond ring on the drummer's finger he quickly slipped it off and insisted she accept it as a present.

Long after the film was completed, Roger said: 'I never get bored with *Tommy*.' Throughout the production he developed a very close relationship with Ken Russell. In the course of filming he had to do many extraordinary things. But even when ordered to 'fly' by Russell, he didn't think twice and just did as he was asked. It was only his second attempt at hang-gliding, but Russell told him he was a sensation and definitely would not die, at least until the movie had been completed. Even four hundred feet up in the air, Roger knew he was perfectly safe. 'It was a bottle job, jumping off a cliff,' he said afterwards. 'But I would do anything for Ken.'

In fact, there was at least one accident with the hang-glider when Roger had to launch himself from a fell in the Lake District and fly down to the watching camera crew. The shot was completed beautifully but he overshot slightly and landed in a field of thistles. Crew members recall hearing loud unscripted expletives, and Roger's ever-caring wife Heather spent the afternoon pulling thistles out of his bare feet. Roger enjoyed the physical aspect of the production, but at times the temperature plummeted so low that stripping off was no fun. 'You never get used to being that cold,' he said. 'It took me three hours to warm up enough to stop shaking.'

At another point during filming Russell asked Roger to remove one shoe and run over a course of several dozen smashed-in and burning pinball machines. 'The film crew are wearing asbestos suits and you are wearing just a tee-shirt but you will not be hurt,' said the director cheerfully. Roger was so enthused he made the run, and survived the experience unhurt.

Indeed, he was determined to undertake most of the many extraordinary stunts in the film himself. That really was him falling backwards through mirrors, getting drenched under a hosepipe and struggling through blazing pinball machines. But he was most definitely not allowed to do the stunt where Tommy leaps off a tall tower. 'They wouldn't insure me to do that,' he said with a rueful grin.

He was always extremely keen that his many fans should both enjoy the new actor Roger Daltrey and appreciate the fierce optimism at the heart of *Tommy*. 'But that is most certainly not the real me up there,' he said. 'That's the only thing I am worried about, that people might think that I really am Tommy. That is one of the strongest reasons for taking new and different roles. I'm not really a "deaf, dumb and blind kid".'

Roger was not the kind of film star to sit isolated in his caravan. He loved being part of a hard-working team and travelling around the country with a single, highly focused purpose in mind. 'Working on *Tommy* certainly gave me the taste for doing more acting,' he said. 'I think it has been good for someone from the pop business to go into it. There are a lot of stories that kids could easily identify with that deserve to be made into films.' He especially enjoyed the concentration of effort: 'There is no social life when you are filming but I like it. The film people really do work and they live for what they are doing, which makes a change these days. With Ken the only thing that is important is the film and he knows the names of all the people, like the chippies. It's a really good atmosphere. It's like being in an enormous pop group on tour. It's good fun.'

And it certainly gave him plenty of food for thought. 'This country must be the worst in the affluent western world for looking after its kids,' he decided. 'When I was on location in Portsmouth with *Tommy* there was a huge council estate with one little youth club for what seemed like 10,000 kids. Is it surprising that they walk around the streets breaking windows?'

Roger spoke out angrily about the lack of new venues for groups. Fortunately, there had been no trouble at the Isle of Wight festival and he was annoyed that the event was not repeated, while football, with all of its attendant violence and civil disorder, continued to be a national obsession. 'It's a weird situation when people put up with football crowds that create so many problems – there's nothing creative in football at all – but music groups get put down all the time. They are often not allowed to hold concerts and there's nowhere for them to play. Pop has a greater audience than football but there is far less of it on television. Most kids would prefer to watch and listen to pop music than football.'

Portsmouth inspired rather different emotions in the production's resident funsters Oliver Reed and Keith Moon. The crew were based in Hayling Island, a nearby holiday resort, and when shooting had finished for the day, Moon persuaded his new best friend to join him in a boat trip across the Solent to the Isle of Wight to visit a friend. After a riotous night out the two returned to Ryde to find the last Portsmouth ferry had long since departed. Reed was concerned as he had a very early call. 'No problem,' said Moon. 'We'll hire a fishing boat.' Some hours later they eventually paid a girl and her father to ferry them back to the mainland in an outsize rowing boat. Reed recalled later: 'It was like Flora MacDonald. The father rowed with the daughter steering. And Keith stood on the prow with all the waves coming over shrieking and shouting at the sea.' By the time the boat approached Hayling Island the sea conditions made it impossible to land. Moon and Reed were forced to strip off and swim the last stretch, and they disturbed the breakfasting film crew with a nude entrance and a demand for warming brandies.

'Keith was always outrageous,' said Roger. 'There was no such thing with him as normal behaviour. You just never knew quite what to expect. He and Oliver Reed formed a great friendship, but they weren't exactly relaxing to have around.'

Tommy was remarkably successful financially. It soon earned back its £1.5-million production costs and went into profit. Ann-Margret's stalwart performance even won her an Oscar nomination, perhaps for her versatility with large quantities of baked beans. But the critics' reactions were mixed, to say the least.

In the *New York Times* Vincent Candy was full of praise for Russell's work: 'Now at long last the man and his method have found a nearly perfect match in subject matter.' But today film is perhaps less well regarded. The *Time Out* film guide rates *Tommy* as one of Ken Russell's 'very worst' films and *Halliwell's Film and Video Guide* calls it a 'mystical rock opera screened with the director's usual barrage of effects and an ear-splitting score. Of occasional interest'.

Whatever the critics felt, *Tommy* was crucial in vastly expanding the career of Roger Daltrey from rock star to film star. The movie may not have been to everyone's taste, but it projected Roger to a cinema-going audience who might not otherwise have been drawn to The Who and their music. The movie pulled in die-hard fans of the band, but it also attracted many who had never been to a concert by The Who and others who had never bought a record by the group. Roger, moreover, now had box office value, and TV and film producers began regarding him in a very different light from merely being the front man of The Who. Roger's raw enthusiasm and his willingness to entrust himself to Ken Russell's artistic whims had pulled him through.

After one success with Ken Russell, Roger was keen to work on the director's new film, *Lisztomania*. With *Tommy* about to go on release, he found himself back in front of the cameras, this time playing the famous composer Franz Liszt as a long-haired, highly sexed cockney. As Roger put it, Liszt was: 'A sort of nineteenth-century Mick Jagger who wanted to get as much upper-class crumpet as he could.'

Roger was by now devoted to Ken Russell. 'He is what I've needed for a long time. He brings things out of me that no one else can. *Tommy* was one thing. I can understand him wanting me to do that, but this Liszt lark! I thought he was kidding when he asked me. I still don't know if I'll be able to act. I still don't. I'll just do as I'm told.' He was very conscious that he had no training as an actor. 'I may not know what I'm up to but I go all passionate in everything I do,' he said. 'For me the best way to work is to go straight in at the deep end.'

When production started on *Lisztomania* it was the only film being made in England. There was only one aspect that gave Roger cause for concern. 'There is some dangerous sword fighting with very sharp swords,' he said, 'and Liszt was supposed to be not very good at it. Somewhere else there is a piano containing some flame throwers. It's so over the top it will either be incredibly successful or a terrible flop.'

Franz Liszt was born on 22 October 1811 in the town of Raiding, which was then in Hungary but after border changes is now in eastern Austria. Even as a child he was a brilliant pianist, and gave his first concert when he was just nine years old. He became a musical superstar of his day, touring Europe with dazzling success and forming friendships with fellow composers like Berlioz, Chopin, Wagner and Mendelssohn, as well as with famous writers like Victor Hugo. Ken Russell built an extraordinary film which was only very loosely based on the facts of the composer's life. In fact, under his direction Roger plays Liszt as a sex maniac who even picks up girls while appearing on the concert platform.

The tone of *Lisztomania* is set right at the start, when we meet Liszt making love to Countess Marie d'Agoult (played by Fiona Lewis) to the mad tick-tock of a relentless metronome. Liszt is surprised by the arrival of the Count, who, not surprisingly, objects to this behaviour and attacks the composer with a sword. The Countess is only mildly disturbed by the fracas and starts eating a banana, only to pause and say casually: 'Don't cut off his genius in its prime.' If this is not bizarre enough, the cheating couple are then seen strapped in a bed shaped like a grand piano and placed on a railway line in front of an oncoming train. After that the film is largely a bizarre sequence of wild behaviour and strange sexual frolics.

This time Ken Russell was in total control of the script and he was determined to portray Franz Liszt and Richard Wagner as the world's first pop stars. Their concert appearances in the movie drew the sort of reaction that Justin Timberlake or Robbie Williams might enjoy today. While Roger is the undoubted star as Liszt, he had terrific support from another *Tommy* actor, Paul Nicholas, who played the turbulent genius Richard Wagner. Princess Carolyn, who was to become the true love of Liszt in his later life, was played by the stunning Royal Shakespeare Company actress Sarah Kestelman. Nineteen-year-old Irish actress Veronica Quilligan played Liszt's wayward daughter Cosima, who deserts her first husband, Hans von Bülow (Andrew Reilly), to marry the charismatic Wagner. John Justin played Countess Marie's cuck-olded husband, who fights a colourful duel with Liszt when he finds him in his wife's bed.

Russell packed the story with eminent composers. Ken Colley played Chopin, Ken Parry was Rossini, Murray Melvin was Berlioz and Andrew Faulds played Johann Strauss. *Lisztomania* showed that the hero of the film had his own early gang of attractive female camp followers, led by Lola Montez (Anulka Dziubinska) and George Sand (Imogen Claire), who were the nineteenth-century equivalent of groupies. Russell even wanted his old favourite Oliver Reed for a guest spot but the actor was unable at the last minute to find time in his busy schedule.

Perhaps Russell's most audacious piece of casting was to include ex-Beatle Ringo Starr as the Pope. He has to visit Liszt, who in later life has become a priest, to tell him that Wagner is now the Prince of Darkness and to order him to use his musical powers to exorcise the devils in Wagner's soul.

If Roger was at times a shade confused during the production of *Tommy*, he felt permanently bamboozled during the making of *Lisztomania*. The slim, 57-page script was really just a general guide and the controversial director as usual carried the complex master plan of the film in his head. Russell certainly used all of the free rein his powerful imagination had been allowed. He was deter-mined to give the musical scene a contemporary feel and at one point even has Liszt say: 'Piss off, Brahms', while at another a miserable Mendelssohn moans: 'Music, schmusic, it's a living, dear boy.' Art director Philip Harrison even managed to recreate a romantic Swiss chalet (inspired by Charlie Chaplin's hut in his 1925 masterpiece *The Gold Rush*) for Liszt's well-known 'Love's Dream', here both given lyrics and sung by Roger Daltrey.

Russell's remarkable screenplay for *Lisztomania* opens in 1830, when the composer was 19, and concludes more than a century later in the ruins of Hitler's Berlin. That is where the Frankenstein's monster figure born of Wagner's music and philosophy is finally destroyed and disappears in flames as Liszt and a body of angels fly off into the infinite heavens.

Liszt gives a virtuoso performance at a concert which drives the audience wild, but he soon gets enveloped in a complex and only occasionally comprehensible plot. This reaches a climax when Cosima deserts her husband, Hans, and renounces her faith to marry Satan himself. The charismatic Richard Wagner has evidently become the Devil himself in his evil climb to power and riches. It is then that the Pope is forced to intervene to order Liszt to cast out the Devil in Wagner. Only by saving his former friend's soul will Liszt redeem his music. Until that task is done it is tainted in the eyes and ears of the world and must remain banned. Liszt sets off to drown Wagner in Holy Water, but he is warned at the doors of Wagner's sinister castle on the banks of the Rhine that he is in great danger from the master's music. Hans refuses to let Liszt in, saying that the music is an evil drug masquerading as a universal cure. But Liszt spots Wagner and Cosima dressed in their ceremonial robes in the Hall of the Ring. Liszt knocks on the window and is allowed in by Wagner. Liszt is taken on a conducted tour of the laboratory where Wagner is creating his superman 'Siegfried', who will become the prototype of the new master race once Wagner's music and philosophy give him life.

Liszt slips Holy Water into Wagner's drink and as Liszt plays his terrifying 'Dance of Death' music, Wagner collapses. But Cosima enters and has her servants lock up Liszt. Trapped in his prison cell, he is put through countless agonies as Cosima plunges a pin into a voodoo doll representing him.

Roger found himself totally exhausted after filming these sequences. 'Most of the time I hadn't a clue what was going on to be honest,' he said. 'Ken Russell is a great director but he was so totally involved with these amazing scenes that I just did what I was told.'

Liszt screams as pain racks his body and furious Cosima angrily holds him responsible for ruining the lives of her and her mother as well as for causing Wagner's death. German soldiers surround Wagner's tomb and a scary figure emerges. Audiences were never quite sure if it was Wagner, Frankenstein or Hitler, or an amalgam of all three. At any rate it is a monster given life by Wagner's music and philosophy and it marches proudly out with Cosima. She presses a final pin through the heart of the doll representing Liszt and the composer drops dead in his cell.

But in Heaven Liszt is happily reunited with all of his women – Maria, Cosima and Carolyn – while back on earth the evil Wagner is destroyed, in the final triumphant sequence of the film, by Liszt, the angels and the power of music.

Roger's memory of the production is of some bitterly cold and wet days of shooting and lots and lots of strange simulated sex. 'It's nice work if you can get it,' he joked to a friend after a particularly raunchy sequence was finally in the can. Russell had him playing six characters who represented various aspects of Liszt's personality.

Roger revelled under Russell's ground-breaking direction. He laughed: 'I spent one whole day on *Lisztomania* vanishing up the left leg of a giant pair of knickers. It seemed a perfectly reasonable thing to do at the time. And in a fencing sequence during which I had to swing from a chandelier with a naked lady I was stabbed twice. I reckon the film business is pretty tough.'

He adds: 'He should have been called Franz Lust because he lusted after everything. There are similarities between Liszt and myself. Did you know that he drew most of his creative energy from women? Playing Liszt was pretty easy. After all Liszt was a raver, and I understand people like that.'

Eventually *Lisztomania* ran five weeks over schedule and the result was almost predictably shocking and controversial. But Roger admitted he was amazed and astonished when he viewed the final version of the film. 'The first time I saw it I was shattered. I wondered what the hell I had done and I knew more or less what was coming. In *Lisztomania* Ken Russell takes the mickey out of porn movies. There is a lot of sex in the film and quite a lot of that was my idea. I am not offended in the least by naked ladies.

'Few people will believe how many of the crazy things in the film are based on fact. Liszt really was a raver. He really was caught in bed with an 18-year-old bird in a monastery and she really did take a shot at him. He really did run off with a countess, have three kids with her, and never marry her. We changed his music a bit but basically it is still his music. I just sort of bluesed it up. Next time I would like to try something dead straight. And that means making a film with another director of course.'

There was one thing Roger took from the film – a ten-foot-tall polystyrene penis, which at one point in the story was Liszt's proudest possession and even served as a celebratory maypole. It was a prop which Roger, with his keen sense of humour, took an instant fancy to, and after filming was over he took it home to Sussex.

Pupils from the local convent school used to pass it on their way home after lessons and found it hugely amusing. But the local residents didn't, and complained *en masse* about this offensive object standing erect in Roger's back garden. Roger's response was to go back to the studio and collect the second giant penis constructed for the film, and so the schoolgirls were amused to see not one but two huge phalluses. Eventually the rain eroded both of them away.

Lisztomania was released in November 1975 and instantly caused a storm of controversy. The protests began even before the public saw the film. The Liszt Society wrote to film critics of their concern at the prospect of their hero being subjected to 'the Ken Russell treatment'. The letter complained: 'Our apprehensions are heightened by the news that the music has been rearranged in rock style and that the story contains scenes of rape, blood sucking, exorcism and castration.' The Society said that while it did not wish to judge the film before it had received a fair viewing, its members really feared that it would show the composer 'in a totally unworthy light'.

As critic Dilys Powell wrote in the *Sunday Times*: 'The Liszt Society didn't know the half of it, yet the whole thing has nothing to do with their Liszt. It is a series of variations on a theme. The theme is the life of Liszt, but it is a life of extravagant myth. As for the Liszt music, what there is of it competes with visual images so bizarre as to defeat any attempt to take its treatment seriously. The film then, is impudent, vulgar, near pornographic. And I like it.' Sadly, she was something of a lone voice, as much of the reaction was negative

Roger was unconcerned. Of the reaction to the film he said at the time: 'Who wants to win a bleedin' Oscar? Not me. I think the film is great and I am 100% behind it. But narrow-minded twits are never going to understand the film and I don't much care. If it makes money, great. If it doesn't then it kept people in work for 16 weeks, so that's all right too. It is certainly not a film that will go unnoticed, and one day it will be regarded as a masterpiece. Ken Russell is ahead of his time. Lots of actors make terrible films that you never hear about, but if you make a terrible Ken Russell film everybody hears about it. We earned a lot of money out of *Tommy* and we are ploughing it back into the industry.'

He was on a high after two starring roles. He realised acting opened up whole new avenues and said: 'The world is so full of things to do. I don't know what I'll do. But I bet your life I'll be doing something I want to do. I take one thing at a time. Life is a very long ladder and I can't see where the next step is. I always wanted to be a successful rock 'n' roll musician. Right, but when you get what you want it's what you do with it, isn't it? There must be something even bigger than being where I am now. Don't ask me what. Ask me when I've done it.'

It's worth noting here that, for all the pleasure he derived from his varied film roles, Roger still values his career in music above all else. 'I've had more chances in my lifetime than most people do if they live to be 90,' he said. 'Whatever happens with acting it will never take the place of singing. Nothing will ever take the place of The Who. Nothing could feel better than being up there in front of real people singing real songs.'

The Who already had plans for a production based on their second rock opera, *Quadrophenia*, as well as Pete Townshend's long-standing project *Lifehouse*. 'It's a kind of futuristic, musical adventure fairytale,' said Roger. And as the seventies drew to a close The Who were working hard on the film *The Kids Are Alright*, a montage of music, film clips and interviews from their music career.

But Roger insisted then that The Who had no thought of retiring as a rock group. They had their first album in two years, *Who Are You*, nearing completion. Of this Roger said: 'It is back to the optimistic, gutsy Who, and not at all pessimistic like *The Who by Numbers*. Although there has always been a danger of The Who disintegrating from the day we started, I think it's less likely to happen now than ever before. We're more together than we've ever been. I see no reason why we shouldn't survive for another ten years.'

Nevertheless, Roger had a taste for acting and his blossoming career as a film star continued with a bizarre cameo role in a horror movie called *The Legacy*, starring Katharine Ross. But his contribution to the film involved little more than dying bloodily and gruesomely at a sinister dinner party when he finds a chicken bone stuck in his throat and one of the other guests attempts to remove it. Roger said: 'It's pretty horrific and very realistic. I've always

Breakthrough: Roger's starring role in *Tommy*, as the deaf, dumb and blind pinball wizard, launched him on a new parallel career as an actor.

Tommy, can you hear me? Ann-Margret's Hollywood expertise and glamour and Roger's raw enthusiasm brought the rock opera *Tommy* alive on screen.

Harping back: Roger looked back to a music star of a different era when he played the composer Franz Liszt in Ken Russell's extraordinary extravaganza *Lisztomania*.

Stolen glance: Roger eyes up the breakfast menu in a scene from the movie *McVicar* in which Roger portrayed the man who was once Britain's most wanted criminal.

Jump to it: Roger struts his stuff in front of manic Keith Moon's arsenal of drums while Pete leaps to strike a chord in mid-air. At their peak The Who were acknowledged as the most exciting live band in the world.

In tune: they have often been antagonists, but Roger and Pete Townshend strive for a harmonious musical relationship in concert.

Brothers in arms: with the Ox, as John Entwhistle was known, and Moon the Loon, who both met premature deaths. Roger insists the spirit of each of them lives on every time he and Pete take the stage as The Who.

And then there were two: grim-faced Roger and Pete Townshend mourn the death of the Ox at John Entwhistle's funeral. John died on the eve of a US tour.

Hello squire: Roger enjoying the essential trappings of rock stardom with a classic motor car at his magnificent mansion in Sussex.

Full bloom: Roger's beautiful wife Heather in the garden of their home set in rolling Sussex countryside. Heather created a stable home environment for Roger to come home to after the madness of The Who on tour.

Reeling and rodding: Roger indulged his lifelong passion for fishing by creating a trout farm at his Sussex home.

Between a rock and a hard place: Roger was happy to rough it when living the life of a pioneering frontiersman for The History Channel's TV series *Extreme History*.

Then: Roger sports a frizzy perm, bare chest and tasselled buckskin jacket to wow the vast peace-and-love hippie crowd at the Isle of Wight Festival in 1969.

And now: a rock veteran with specs appeal at the age of 60, Roger energetically shows a new generation of Who fans why they are still headliners 35 years later at the Isle of Wight Festival in 2004.

The kids are alright: Roger with his wife Heather and their children Rosie, Willow and Jamie on a family night out.

wanted to be in a horror film. It was great fun. I want to go into films seriously later on, but I need experience. And the only way to get experience is to go out there and do it.'

The Who moved into movies as record sales were declining. Without any grand announcements the group wrote, produced and financed *Quadrophenia*, which was premiered in August 1979 and closely followed by *The Kids Are Alright*.

But Roger's dramatic imagination was by then dominated by playing colourful criminal John McVicar, a man who had been released on parole in 1978 after serving 11 years of a 26-year sentence for armed robbery. He had been fascinated ever since hearing McVicar described by Scotland Yard as 'the most dangerous man in Britain'.

'From the time I first met John McVicar I was struck by the idea of making a film about him,' he said. So much of McVicar's life and battles with authority seemed to mirror Roger's own feelings and attitudes. 'We both went through the same kind of adolescent fantasies. At 15 I had the same feelings of ego. Like him I wanted money. I wanted to be the Face, the King Pin – have the flashest car. And I was a street fighter. I found my way to all that through pop music. I did not need to sit in a getaway car outside a bank to make the adrenalin flow. It happened to me on stage.'

He had instantly seen massive similarities between his life and McVicar's. They were both determined to break out from a boring, dead-end existence. 'Fortunately I found that being in a group was a great release,' he said. 'McVicar got out the only way he knew how – through crime. If it hadn't been for rock 'n' roll I would probably have been a real-life John McVicar.'

Roger bought the film rights to the autobiography McVicar wrote in jail. He knew intuitively that it would be a powerful and compelling movie and he always planned to play the title role himself. 'You would be surprised how alike we look when my hair is cut short,' he said. 'Once everything is absolutely definite (about the production) I hope to meet McVicar face to face.' He wrote to the

Home Office and asked for permission to visit him. Characteristically, Roger became passionate about the project and insisted that the film would not try to whitewash McVicar in any way. 'He himself does not set out to do that in his book. But the film might help to explain what happened to him.'

Work began on *McVicar* at Shepperton Studios in June 1979. The Who owned a large slice of the complex thanks to a £2-million investment from record royalties. With touching enthusiasm Roger said: 'It is more fun putting your money into something like that than moving it to the Bahamas or perhaps doing something illegal in Switzerland.'

McVicar opened in August 1980. The *Sun*'s film critic Kit Miller insisted it would be 'criminal' to miss it and acclaimed Roger's performance as 'brilliant'. 'The film, based on a true story, follows the malicious misfortunes of one of Britain's hardest criminals, a rugged rogue who refused to give in to the system.' Inside prison Roger looked totally different from the wild man of rock: slimmed down, his famous long hair cut off, his cheeks sunken and his eyes wild and staring. Questions about his acting ability might have remained after the musical extravaganzas *Tommy* and *Lisztomania,* but with *McVicar* Roger appeared to have sentenced himself to a long film career. Particularly memorable were the steamy scenes with Georgina Hale.

Roger's flirtation with the gangster world for *McVicar* had a profound impact on him. He developed a fear of being followed by real-life gangsters who might have felt some injustice over something in the film. He confessed his fears to magistrates at Sevenoaks in Kent when facing a speeding charge for driving his Ferrari at 115mph, for which he was fined £100. He also admitted that his colourful lifestyle meant that he was in constant danger from jealous boyfriends.

For a while Roger was certainly identified with the more dangerous side of life, and when Jonathan Miller was looking for someone to play 'a bad man with vast sexual potential' in a BBC production of *The Beggar's Opera* in 1983, the director went straight to him. It turned into an inspired choice, for Roger's performance as the roguish highwayman Macheath was crucial to the success of the film.

From the start Miller went for authenticity. He even decided to rehearse with Hogarth's drawings, which were inspired by the original production, laid out in front of the cast. The director felt this was one opera which simply could not be updated. 'It is rooted in its own pastoral time and every melody carries the smell of those green London fields,' he said. Miller didn't want Macheath as a jovial highwayman full of twinkling roguishness and nudge-nudge 'Carry On' gallantry. In his opinion, what John Gay had had in mind 200 years earlier when he wrote the play was 'an intense, bad man who is sexually fantastically plausible, but at the same time perfectly capable of cutting throats. Rock musician Roger Daltrey was exactly the Macheath I'd hoped – while giving him his head one found oneself quite green with envy at his success with women and all the groping he was allowed.'

Yet initially the signs were not good. Roger insists he 'hates' opera. 'And I had never even heard of *The Beggar's Opera* until I got a call from the producer, Jonathan Miller. He sent me a copy of the record. God, it was awful. I told him I couldn't possibly sing like that.' He said, "Don't worry, it's all right. That's exactly what I don't want you to do. I want you to be yourself." So I decided to give it a go.' For his part, Miller said: 'I saw Roger in the film *McVicar* and I thought he was just perfect for Macheath. He plays him like a south London villain.'

The role of Macheath is one with which Roger could identify: 'He is the ultimate lecher where women are concerned. I have been like him in the past but not now.' Before the film was screened he expressed his concern for Heather: 'It must have been hard for her to watch me groping all those birds. I would have hated to watch her if she was in the same situation. In fact, all the women who have seen it so far at previews have come out with a twinkle in their eye as if I was going to leap on them. In that respect the creation of an image in rock music and acting is not all that different. I used to get myself mentally right to play a part on stage with The Who and after a show Heather would say to me, "You are not the same bloke who comes home with me in the car. Worse luck!"'

He added, laughing: 'I sometimes felt strange being a rock 'n' roll star at my age, especially as the audiences were getting younger. Yet with acting I feel great. More confident for a start. I have a burning passion for it and I'm learning all the time.

'When Jonathan first asked me to play Macheath, I listened to the existing recording he sent and thought, well, I hope he does not want all that Pretty Polly plumminess because that is not me at all. I tried it out instead in my own gravel-path cockney and I felt it could work. Then, talking to Jonathan, I realised with relief that what he was after was Macheath in a torn and filthy jacket, the sort of character who survives on the knife edge of the wrong side of the law and who can't stay away from the birds. What is it – half a dozen wives by the end and heaven knows how many women of the town!'

He told Miller that, rather like Gay himself, he didn't care for opera. 'The bits I have seen on television don't communicate to me. It's all too stiff and there are too many conventions about the action stopping for the singer to face front and stretch out his arms before bursting into song. It seems to me that life is an opera – you walk past a building site and there are the men finding it perfectly natural to work and sing at the same time. It was great that Jonathan wanted to play *The Beggar's Opera* as if it really were life – moving straight from dialogue and business into a song and back again.'

As evidenced by his commitment to tell McVicar's story, Roger was intrigued by the criminal mentality and the plight of finding oneself, like Macheath, suddenly behind bars. 'I've had a taste of prison myself, after wild parties in wrecked hotel rooms, and it really is a most terrifying affront to your liberty. You feel reduced to well, totally nothing, you're just a bit of life's flotsam floating helplessly.'

The Beggar's Opera was very well received, but Roger hardly had time to relax before he was plunged into another dramatic first – Shakespeare. For a prestigious production of *The Comedy of Errors* boasting names like Dame Wendy Hiller, Cyril Cusack, Charles Gray, Michael Kitchen and Ingrid Pitt, the former wild man of The Who was approached to audition for the parts of the twin servants the Dromos. In modern productions of Shakespeare not all actors use the traditional pronunciation. Roger's marked London accent perfectly fitted the Dromos' lowly social status. So he didn't have to learn the rhythm of Shakespeare's verse, even though that would have been a fairly easy task for such an accomplished musician.

Roger was certainly determined to get the role. 'My agent sent me along to read for it,' he said. 'I spent five hours studying the book with a dictionary on one knee. At school, Acton County Grammar, I hated Shakespeare. We never acted the plays. They were part of our English lesson. The master did not do a good job of explaining, either.'

He was keen to impress the play's director, James Cellan Jones, and happily underwent what was his very first audition. To Roger's credit there was no big-star reaction to the idea of taking a test. 'Why should I be any different?' he said. 'Life can't be all ups. If you never come down you'll never know where the ups are.'

Roger was elated when he landed the part. 'I'm more excited about getting this role than receiving my first Gold record,' he said, even though the payment was 'paltry'. 'I wish I was better read and had the time to absorb Shakespeare,' he said, as the experience had opened up a whole new world for him. 'For me it is like having a giant box of toys to play with at 39 years of age. And for that I'm grateful.' When *The Comedy of Errors* was transmitted he said: 'It's my first Shakespeare and I've really got the taste for it now.'

As Roger approached his fortieth birthday, in March 1984, he joked: 'If you want to send me a present I would like a nice giant cream cake with a six foot redhead inside please.' He went on: 'I must admit I feel a bit numb about being so old but I don't worry about it at all. I ache a bit in the morning but basically someone up there must like me. I think the key to feeling good is working from the inside out. If you eat healthy food and look after yourself then it doesn't matter how old you are.'

After *McVicar*, Roger had continued to ponder the lives of criminals who live outside normal society. Indeed he happily admits to having a lifelong fascination with the subject and for many years he campaigned to get the Kray twins released from jail. He regularly visited Ronnie in Broadmoor and Reggie in Parkhurst. Their story was another great British crime film waiting to be made and for years it was a project close to his heart.

With the benefit of hindsight, he was unhappy with his experience in *McVicar* and later dismissed the film as 'one-dimensional and too cops and robbers'. What he now wanted was to make a movie on the Krays that was much more broadly based and realistic, and he worked hard to realise this ambition. Having set the project in motion, he took charge of it and worked energetically at supervising the scripting and casting. He also planned to direct the film himself.

'I'm fighting tooth and nail to get this the way I want it,' he said. 'It's not a gangster film and I don't think it is a subject which will only be of interest to British audiences. Ronnie was a paranoid schizophrenic, and gay, who had an extraordinary relationship with his mother. When Reggie the straight twin fell in love with a girl, Ronnie was very disturbed about that. Reggie later married the girl, who later commits suicide. It is an extraordinary story. And nobody really looked at that relationship between identical twins except for Shakespeare.'

Roger was determined to research his film as fully as possible and when he visited Ronald Kray in Broadmoor to get his comments, he found him possessed of a 'frightening charisma'. 'But then that's why people are fascinated by criminals, isn't it?' he said. 'It's like going to see the tigers at the zoo. I don't excuse what the Krays did, and I did tell Ronnie that he wasn't going to come out of this looking too good.'

His firm belief was that, whatever the public view, the Krays were a part of our folk history. He found Ronnie coherent and still very humorous rather than crazy. And even sitting opposite him, knowing he had killed people, he found he could not help but warm to him. Roger was amazed by the way so many self-righteous people refused to have anything to do with the project simply because of the Krays' reputation. He accepted that Ronnie was a psychopath and that the twins murdered people. But he insisted that the people the Krays murdered were other villains.

Both brothers fascinated him. 'Their psychology is far more interesting than that of someone like Al Capone. The very fact that they are twins with a complex relationship makes them far more interesting than any other gangsters I can think of.'

However, despite all of Roger's dedicated work, a mass of logistical complications intervened, with the result that by 1987 he had reluctantly handed over control of his pet project. 'It's a fabulous story,' he said. 'But it won't be the movie I wanted to make – it'll be a gangster film.' The film went into production in October 1987 with veteran director Franc Roddam directing and Roger taking a back seat as associate producer. He felt let down certainly, but his response at the time was predictably pragmatic: 'I want to get it made and I'm letting it go this way otherwise I'll lose it completely.'

At the same time Roger remained in demand as an actor, having established his credentials in film and on stage. In October 1984 he starred with Toyah Willcox, Terry Raven and Leslie Ash in *Murder: Ultimate Grounds For Divorce*, a sadly forgettable thriller about two couples on a camping holiday on the south coast of England.

Two years later he starred alongside Twiggy in *The Little Match Girl*, ITV's Christmas production of Hans Christian Anderson's weepy classic story. Eleven-year-old Natalie Morse played the tragic role of the child match seller who freezes to death in the grim streets of London's East End in the 1890s. The production was cruelly written off as over-sentimental, but Roger scarcely cared. 'I loved working with Twiggy,' he said. 'I've always admired her. I'm always ready to consider any script sent to me. It's nice to be working, even if it's nothing special. Such is the working life of an actor.' He disagreed with the sneering verdict of the critics and was adamant that the lavish, 90-minute musical production contained a hard-hitting message, pointing out the ills and warped moral values of Victorian society.

All the same he seemed much more at ease in Mike Batt's highly enjoyable musical version of Lewis Carroll's *The Hunting of the Snark*. He played the Barrister in an imaginative treatment of the famous poem which also drew fine performances from Billy Connolly, Justin Hayward and Midge Ure.

But Roger often seemed happier still in tougher roles. In 1988 he landed one in a TV movie called *Gentry* which shocked viewers at the time. The story featured a solicitor (Duncan Preston) being battered in the head and stomach with a pump-action shotgun and his pregnant wife (Phoebe Nicholls) being brutally assaulted. He played a hardened criminal who holds a young couple to ransom while trying to track down a missing £1.7 million.

Roger insisted that the scenes were not too violent, but it was hard to believe this was supposed to be a comedy drama. The laughs definitely took a back seat as his character, Colin, broke into the young couple's home and tormented them with a memorable degree of menace. Roger said: 'It'll probably shock someone, but I'll have no qualms letting my children see it. I do look pretty horrific but there's a lot of black humour in it. Besides there's far worse on the box at the moment. I'm a jobbing actor and I can't afford to turn down roles.'

Colin was a gang leader who had received horrific injuries in a car crash. Make-up girl Linette Braid spent days in a hospital's casualty unit trying to find just the right look. Roger was excellent, as usual, but the story's intimidating violence did create controversy. He defended the film because it looked realistically at aggression. 'There is violence in all of us but it just comes out in different forms,' he said.

All the same, Roger was delighted to switch to a lighter role as the central figure of Cashman in ITV's three-hour comedy series *How to Be Cool.* Cashman was a sinister Mr Big of the fashion world, 'all dark suits and dark glasses'. He ran the National Cool Board and 'decided what's in and what's out. He dictated fashion and decided whether it's cool to wear mini-skirts or white socks or whatever and determines the width of your lapel.'

Roger insisted his fanatical, fashion-crazed character was nothing like him because he had never been remotely interested in clothes. 'I get Heather to buy my gear for me,' he said. 'I hate shopping and I'm proud to say I've never set foot in Harrods. I'm a jeans and T-shirt man. Heather buys my stuff and what I don't like goes back. Anyway at only five feet seven inches tall, clothes don't look that good on me. I look like a bag of wet laundry in the eighties fashions. I liked sixties clothes, they were straightforward. Punk was the same, clean lines, not the mess you get today.'

A bunch of kids led by former *Coronation Street* actress Gina Seddon set out to expose this evil organisation, enlisting the help of a TV producer played by Gary Glitter. 'It's shot like a pop video,' said Roger. 'There is lots of music and it's very fast and very exciting. I don't go after tough-guy roles. I would love to play a romantic lead, but I take what I am offered.'

And he continued to be offered a great deal. His portrayal of the Street Singer for Menahem Golan's *Mack the Knife* saw him return to the story of *The Beggar's Opera* even though the production was a great deal less faithful to the source material than Miller's BBC version. This time Raul Julia played Macheath and most viewers felt Roger's earlier performance was not surpassed.

All the time Roger's enthusiasm for acting grew and grew. 'It all started with *Tommy* but that was really singing, so I could handle that. But when I did *Lisztomania* I suddenly realised I was totally out of my depth and I didn't know the first thing about acting. I know I looked silly. I decided to do any bit of acting, videos, short films, Shakespeare for the BBC for nothing, anything for experience. I didn't go to drama school because I know they are a disaster. They can teach technique but they can't teach you how to act.'

And Roger was never simply prepared to wait patiently for good and challenging roles to come along. With his long experience of show business he was quite happy to wander into production areas in order to make things happen. *Buddy's Song* was a good example. Roger invested a small fortune in the production. He produced it with the same team that made *Quadrophenia* and *McVicar*. He gathered £2.5million from backers, reduced his own fees as star and producer in exchange for a healthy share of the profits and pressed ahead with the project just when the British film industry seemed moribund.

Filmed in 1989 and screened in March 1991, *Buddy's Song* came at a difficult time for Britain's film business, as Roger explained: 'When we started shooting *Buddy's Song* it was the only feature film in production in England. That's how bad things are. But I'm enjoying producing a film at the time when others aren't because the industry is on its knees.

'*Buddy's Song* is unashamedly British. I'm very proud it's not Hollywood glitz. It deals intelligently with real problems. I'm very proud of it.'

The film was based on a television series Roger acted in for the schools programmes on BBC2 in 1986. This series, itself based on Nigel Hinton's award-winning novel, told the story of a father who is a Teddy boy and a Buddy Holly fan who turns his son on to the singer. The parents' relationship is breaking up and the son, named after his father's hero, tries to keep the marriage together. The teenage Buddy writes all his feelings into songs. The roles are now reversed, so that the youngster is telling his dad what to do and his dad is just a lunatic Teddy boy. The dad is more of an adolescent than his son, and can be difficult, childish and temperamental. Buddy is shocked to find his father in bed with a woman 20 years younger than his mum.

'I can totally relate to that,' said Roger. 'I've got no identity crisis about playing the dad. It's a great part and it doesn't bother me that I'm the old one this time. But we can't fudge the playing or the acting so it's going to be difficult finding someone to play my son.'

So the search was on. The producers had talent scouts out looking in drama schools and music clubs and pubs for someone who looked good, sang well, played great guitar and was 17 but could play 15. The singing was live in the film, so Roger was convinced miming would not work. Young singer Chesney Hawkes, the son of Chip Hawkes from the sixties group the Tremeloes, got the role and Roger was delighted: 'In Chesney we found the perfect Buddy who can sing wonderfully and, considering he has done no acting before, he has turned in an incredible performance.'

Roger wanted the film to show kids growing up who don't know where the songs come from but who will learn that there's someone out there going through everything they're going through and writing it down. In some ways it made him feel frustrated. He wanted to be starting all over again himself. 'Rock 'n' roll gives you a great excuse to behave like an idiot and live out all your fantasies,' he said, laughing.

The part of the father, Terry, was one Roger found very easy to identify with. He was then 45 and he enjoyed a remarkably liberated attitude towards fatherhood. 'I totally accept the fact that my kids have their own lives to lead. I try to explain to them how things are, but what they do with that advice is their decision. My eldest daughter has a boyfriend now and is very much in charge of her own life. But I have no feelings of fatherly possessiveness when she has boyfriends.'

It was the sort of work that Roger relished. He cheerfully admitted that acting kept him on the straight and narrow. 'I like the discipline,' he said. 'I don't think many people realise how easy it would be for me to become an alcoholic for example. It's a constant battle I fight all the time and I'm very aware of it. But I have lost so many friends through excess.'

Buddy's Song was well received by the critics. The *Sun*'s Sue Evison said: 'Roger Daltrey turns in a good performance as ageing rock 'n' roller Terry Clark. He is desperate to relive his youth through his talented musician son Buddy, played by Chesney Hawkes. Michael Elphick is wonderfully cringe-making as Terry's shady pal Des. And Sharon Duce is excellent as Terry's wife Carol who refuses to be downtrodden. Hawkes' performance is promising but self-conscious. He seems slightly overwhelmed by Daltrey. You feel he's dying to ask him for his autograph. The story is slow to start though it eventually gains pace. But this kitchen sink drama is not pretending to be one of the great. It's simply a heart-warming tale of family strife with a big dose of fun thrown in. And if you like a bit of rip roaring rock 'n' roll you will love this movie.'

But otherwise this was a difficult time for Roger. In March 1991 he announced he was quitting music for good after eight years of trying to make it on his own without The Who. He decided he no longer wanted to be regarded as a lone rocker and planned to concentrate on acting instead. But he still felt keenly the loss of the band. 'I miss the camaraderie, the performing and Pete Townshend,' he explained. 'As soon as Pete was taken from me so was my existence, my lifeblood. I love singing but not the hassle of putting the show on. I was really just a virtuoso singer for Pete Townshend's music. It was very frustrating because I still want to play with the group but Pete doesn't.'

At the same time he admitted he found it difficult to come to terms with his movie career. 'I still have not got to grips with sitting down and doing nothing but waiting for months. I start thinking, God, the world's coming to an end. I wish I didn't worry so much I get quite woeful. I also get frustrated and think, what have I achieved?'

But at least the acting work was showing no sign of drying up. He was still in demand all over the world and he made his television acting debut in the States in an episode of *Midnight Caller*, playing a failed rocker. 'I get to sing in the show but I'll probably have to wait a year to see it here,' he said.

Cold Justice was a film that was also made in America, but it didn't start out that way. It started life as a story called *Father Jim*, written by top writer and director Terry Green about two men, a Catholic priest and a down-on-his-luck ex-professional boxer who was reduced to fighting in non-licensed bouts. Dennis Waterman's East End Films switched the project from London to Chicago to attract more American backing. Waterman was originally pencilled in to play the fighter but he decided that he much preferred the dramatic challenges of the priest. But the character was changed so that instead of playing a Scottish priest in London, Waterman became an English priest who turns up in Chicago. The title was changed to *Cold Justice*, but the film was not a success. Waterman was forced to remortgage his house and said bleakly afterwards: 'Apart from the money the really annoying thing about the whole exercise was that the film was crap. I haven't even got a copy. One hears about people taking big risks to make movies and losing their shirt, but at least they emerge with the compensation of artistic credibility. We just lost our money.'

In fact, Roger Daltrey was the best thing in *Cold Justice*. His performance as Keith the Thief was impressive, especially when he stood bruised and battered during a gruesome bare-knuckle fight. He spent weeks training with a boxing coach for his role as the fighter making a comeback. And Waterman, co-starring as the hard-drinking priest, was stunned by Roger's performance. 'It was amazing,' he said. 'The fight is very important to the film and he put his heart and soul into it. At the end he was supposed to collapse on to his stool but he fell flat on his face instead! He thought it would look better and he got a standing ovation from the crew.'

The reception for Paul Hogan's cowboy movie *Lightning Jack* was rather less euphoric. Roger was reduced to a minor role in this film featuring Hogan and Cuba Gooding Junior as a pair of less than slick bank robbers. He did get top billing when he switched to television to star as seventeenth-century seaman explorer William Dampier in a £10-million TV mini-series called *Pirate Tales.* The accent might have shivered more than a few critical timbers but the series sold well around the world.

Roger became a surprise convert to the music of Sir Andrew Lloyd Webber after he starred in a BBC2 production of *Jesus Christ Superstar.* He said: 'I didn't actually like the musical, but I really wanted to play the role of Judas as I think he is a fascinating character. After all without Judas we might not have had Christianity. When it first came out I thought, being a real rock star, this is public schoolboy stuff, but now I have been working on it I have to say I am beginning to like it.'

Being a millionaire with a relatively modest ego was always a great asset to Roger and his acting career. He could afford to take parts which interested him rather than confine himself to 'career-building roles'. He thoroughly enjoyed himself playing an alarming-looking character called 'the Assassin', with long fingernails and bad teeth, in a highly enjoyable episode of *The New Adventures of Superman.* One of Roger's heroines was film star Bette Davis and years previously he had been thrilled to meet her in Los Angeles. 'Now there is a real lady,' he said. 'I would like to have the sort of career she had – where everything she did was for a reason and she was proud of it and she never did anything just for the money.'

Some international superstars might well turn their noses up at a guest appearance in the long-running British crime series *The Bill,* but not Roger. In July 1999 he starred as former drug dealer Lenny Moore. And he took it every bit as seriously as every other role he has approached. 'It has been a thoroughly challenging shoot because the scenes I have been doing are so intense. The character I play is in total despair and I've really beaten myself up to play this role. I needed to dig deep inside myself to play this character.'

Roger's wicked sense of humour makes him always up for a slice of self-parody. He was amused to land a part as an alcoholic rock star in an American sitcom called *Rude Awakenings*, playing opposite Lynn Redgrave. And at the time the old question about acting versus singing raised its head yet again. When he appeared in a version of *Oliver!* at Robert Redford's Sundance Festival in August 1999 he came up with an articulate answer. 'Until I can come up with something that sounds completely different I don't want to make an album,' he said, considering his words carefully. 'It would have to be something that surprised me. I'd hate to make a record that made people ask "Why?" I'm a singer who acts when I'm out of work and an actor who sings when I can't get a gig. I can't just sit around doing nothing. I've got limited talent but volumes of ambition.'

He was even prepared to do panto, and loved appearing in *A Christmas Carol* in New York in 1998. 'I like the stage business and I'm just lucky to be successful,' he said. He earned a string of good reviews except from the *Washington Post's* Tony Kornheiser, who sneered: 'Why do we ask ageing rock stars to embarrass us by acting in a heart-warming musical?'

Roger's enthusiasm for the supernatural led him to accept the role of rogue vampire Vlad in the film *Vampirella*, where he was eventually hunted down by the beautiful Talisa Soto in the skimpiest of sci-fi outfits. And later he appeared in the American TV series *Witchblade* as a priest desperate to get his hands on a mysterious artefact which gives amazing powers to a New York policewoman.

But his great unfulfilled dramatic ambition is to make a film of the life of his eccentric friend Keith Moon. He is determined to provide a colourful, warts-and-all account of the drummer's astonishing story, but it is proving a desperately difficult subject to bring to the screen. For years Roger has nurtured his dream, but the project has seen many false dawns. There have been talks with Mike Myers about his portraying Keith in the film. The comedy genius behind *Wayne's World* and Austin Powers is a Who fan and desperate to play one of his heroes. And that is certainly one of the options. Roger acknowledges that Myers is a comic genius, but he insists: 'The film will happen when it's right and not before. People think it's very easy: oh yeah, great idea, make a film of Keith Moon's life. But biographical films are the most difficult to tackle. Keith was such an enormous personality it would be a bit of everything. The thing about him is that he was the ultimate of everything. He invented the book about how to be a rock 'n' roll lunatic and everybody else has done a copy. It must have been Hell to actually be Keith Moon. How do you have a day off?'

Of course, with a series of books and countless newspaper and magazine articles about him, everyone thinks they know the Keith Moon story already. The Rolls-Royce in the swimming pool is a part of showbiz history and so is the time Moon put a Ferrari engine into a milk float. 'But there was so much more to Keith than that,' insists Roger. 'You know he had a wife and kid: he wasn't just Mr Bonkers. I want to make this film because I've never met anyone like Keith. I see his life as a tragic love story. Keith had this self-destruct element in his nature. He had a mental disorder towards the end. He was the best mimic I've ever seen but his impersonations – of Adolf Hitler, say – began to last for days. But I loved the man very much.' Nonetheless he is determined not to whitewash his old pal and warns there will be parts of the film people will find distasteful. 'But I have promised Keith's family it will be a film where people will come out loving the guy,' says Roger.

Keith was desperately troubled by the death of his 24-year-old chauffeur Cornelius Boland. He would wake up in the middle of the night screaming and sweating at the memory of that night-mare. To people who knew him, Keith was the funniest person imaginable, yet the sad clown tried at least four times to commit suicide but failed miserably each time. Fantasy and reality were so mixed up in his life that he had difficulty separating one from the other. He could be hysterically funny or devastatingly tragic. Tears followed laughter so furiously with Keith that it was impossible to work out what was serious and what was not.

Roger has bought the rights to Keith Moon's story and has spo-ken about the project to the drummer's mother, wife and daughter. But Roger and Pete Townshend, who holds all the rights to the music, are adamant that they will only allow it to go ahead when they are fully satisfied with the scripts. At least three versions of the story have been written and rejected and the list of stars allegedly lined up to play Moon includes Ewan McGregor, Robert Downey Junior and Robbie Williams, to name just a few.

Roger insists it will happen one day but he and Pete are naturally ultra-cautious about the project because to a great extent Keith Moon's story is their story too.

Not that Roger has too many gaps in his busy schedule these days. His particular star status seems to register with fans young and old all over the world and it brings with it some intriguing work offers. History is one of his many passions. He's an avid reader about the past, with a vast self-taught knowledge about many different periods. So he was absolutely delighted when the prestigious History Channel asked him to front *Extreme History* in 2003. This was much more than just a conventional job of TV pre-senter. The channel wanted Roger to go back in time and take on the challenges of some of history's epic adventures, explorations and battles. 'It was the most exciting offer I'd had in ages,' he said. 'It was like getting paid to do something you would like to do for fun.'

Roger was selected because of his international profile and because of his genuine enthusiasm for the past. Each week, on a series that was to find millions of devoted fans right around the world, he met a team of experts who showed him historical techniques for survival. Roger, and through him the viewers, learned how people navigated extreme terrain, weathered hard and unforgiving climates and survived on anything they could kill or gather. Information about events from the pasts was fed into the programmes to try to provide a realistic view of what life was really like in years gone by. Roger was asked to dig trenches, run rapids, scale cliffs one-handed, rope cattle and eat some of the strangest food imaginable. It was a scary challenge but one he was delighted to accept.

'It was all very well researched,' he said. 'And I learned a lot, even if sometimes the going got pretty tough.' Some of the reconstructions were pretty hairy. Back in 1869 Civil War veteran Major John Wesley Powell, who lost an arm in the fighting, almost lost his life trying to map America's final frontier. Powell and his small expedition set out to chart the beautiful and dangerous Colorado River. Even with today's state-of-the-art equipment, it's a treacherous trip. Against the stunning backdrop of Utah's red-rock mesas, Roger recreated this harrowing mission in a wooden replica of Powell's boat. Trying his best not to smash into rocks, he navigated raging rapids. And just like Powell, he scaled 300-foot cliffs using only one arm.

The response from viewers was remarkable and Roger was delighted. 'History is about people doing amazing things,' he said. 'It should never be boring and this show was definitely never that.' He started to win over new fans with some of the feats he performed in the series. He even followed in the footsteps of Lewis and Clark's famous expedition in search of a water route to the Pacific Ocean. They never found it, but along the way they discovered an America that few Europeans had ever seen.

In Wyoming, Roger discovered how Plains Indians lived and died on the trail of the buffalo. One skill he had to learn was how to strip a bloody buffalo hide and turn it into a blanket. He even fastened on his spurs and strapped on a Colt 45 for a lesson in authentic gunfighting, dispelling a few Hollywood myths along the way. 'It was fabulous,' he said. 'Just like being a kid again.'

The range of this imaginative series was impressive. Roger even went prehistoric in one programme, as *Extreme History* recreated early man's survival story. Experts taught him mankind's earliest survival techniques. He learned how to fashion history's first tools, and how to make fire and a weapon to hunt with. 'In order to make history, the first thing you have to do is survive it,' said Roger, who really threw himself into the project.

He even got to relive one of the most ignominious defeats in British history as he found out what life was like on board the American brig *Niagara*. This battleship was commanded by Oliver Hazard Perry in his defeat of the British in the Battle of Lake Erie in 1813. It was the first time in the history of the Royal Navy that an entire fleet surrendered in battle. But then the presenter flashed forward in time to explore the history of sports-car racing in deepest Georgia. 'It was a fabulous ride,' he said. 'But then so was the whole series.'

Millions of viewers around the world loved *Extreme History*, but many wondered why a millionaire rock star would put himself through such punishing stunts. Roger explained: 'I have been coming to America for almost 40 years. I've probably been across it more times than most Americans but I've seen virtually none of the real country. I've seen the inside of a lot of limos, lots of hotel rooms, concert halls and stadiums, but I've never seen the bits of America that I'd always wanted to see. So this was a really good opportunity. It's been fantastic.' His enthusiasm for history, which came over so strongly on screen, was genuine, he insisted. 'I feel very strongly that the only way to make history grab a new audience is to bring something new to it. I love history yet at school it was the most boring thing I've ever sat through in my whole life. All they wanted to talk about was numbers and dates. It was never about people. On this series we take history very seriously but it's not a history lesson in the traditional sense. Some of the experiences I wouldn't have missed for the world. Seeing a fully dressed Sioux Indian in his war paint and feathers riding across the prairie was like seeing a Greek mythological figure come to life. It was absolutely outstanding. I'll carry that memory forever.'

But there were some dangerous moments as well, like the time Roger put on a wolf skin to disguise himself and went hunting wild buffalo with rubber-tipped arrows from just 30 yards away. 'Looking back,' he smiled, 'that was bloody crazy. I've been around animals for 30 years but buffalo are not exactly cattle. There was no way I could have outrun them if they'd turned on me. I was wearing stupid cowboy boots.'

In *Extreme History*, Roger appeared thoroughly at ease in front of the camera – a far cry from his first TV appearances in the 1960s, when The Who were climbing to stardom. Back then he regarded TV as a barrier to what The Who did best, which was giving live, in-your-face performances. He felt uncomfortable in TV studios, so out of place, and was racked with nerves. Rather than a feeling of exhilaration, TV appearances brought Roger terror. 'Stark raving bloody terror' is how he described it in an insightful interview filmed for Reel 2 of the DVD version of the rockumentary *The Kids Are Alright*. 'It wasn't my bag,' he reflected, pointing out that the singer was always live whereas the backing track could be done in the studio by the band whether they were drunk or sober and if they made a mistake it could be reworked again and again. 'The poor old singer,' he lamented, 'had usually been up till four in the morning the night before gigging somewhere up in Scotland and then wheeled down to the studio almost in pieces – I'd be doing it live and it was always terror for me.'

But that was then and in the middle of filming *Extreme History*, Roger felt comfortable enough with the way it was going to take time off to make an appearance in a one-night-only performance of the musical *My Fair Lady* at the Hollywood Bowl in Los Angeles.

Roger had been just 12 years old and starting to show a real interest in music when Alan Jay Lerner's and Frederick Loewe's Broadway masterpiece became the talk of theatreland when launched in New York in 1956.

The show subsequently came to London and ran at the Drury Lane theatre for five and a half years, in the process implanting in the nation's consciousness, including that of young Roger, many of the musical's wonderful songs, such as 'With a Little Bit of Luck', 'Wouldn't It Be Loverly', 'The Rain in Spain' and 'I Could Have Danced All Night'.

Based on Bernard Shaw's play *Pygmalion*, which caused a sensation when first premiered in London in 1916, *My Fair Lady* told the story of the wealthy London gentleman Henry Higgins, an irascible confirmed bachelor, who bets his companion Colonel Pickering that he can take Eliza Doolittle, an ordinary cockney flower seller, and pass her off in high society just by teaching her to 'speak like a lady'. This he does in triumphant fashion, but only after much hard work and frustration and some delicate negotiations with Eliza's father, Alfred P. Doolittle, a drunken London dustman and moralist.

Incongruous as it might at first have seemed for Roger to appear in *My Fair Lady*, the offer of the role of Alfred P. Doolittle was just too tempting to resist. He loved the music and he loved the book and he was not afraid to say so. In 1964, just as The Who were starting to take off, the movie version of *My Fair Lady*, starring Rex Harrison and Audrey Hepburn, became the most eagerly awaited cinematic event since *Gone with the Wind*. Musicals were big box office at that time and *My Fair Lady* was one of the real treats of the era – and it set the nation singing many of its fine songs all over again.

Now Roger had the chance to take a part in a stage production of what was broadly considered *the* musical of the twentieth cen-

tury and one of the most successful shows in the history of musical
theatre, and he jumped at it. He had played the Tin Man in a
Lincoln Centre production of *The Wizard of Oz* in 1995, and three
years later he had appeared in a production of *A Christmas Carol* at
Madison Square Garden. But for Roger, this production of *My
Fair Lady* had the added attraction of being just a one-off performance, which appealed to his gypsy nature of constantly moving
on. Later he would turn down the offer of a stage role in *Chitty
Chitty Bang Bang* because he feared he would get bored in a long
run. 'The longest run The Who did was a five-day stint at Madison
Square Garden,' he pointed out.

Roger was hired just eight weeks before the curtain went up on
My Fair Lady and he had only ten days in which to work on his
role, which included one of the musical's best-loved and most
memorable songs, 'Get Me to the Church on Time'. He saw the
musical as a great study of Edwardian morality, with Alfred P.
Doolittle quite content to be poor. 'Americans find it very difficult
to understand the English class system, but money doesn't buy you
out of it,' he told the *Los Angeles Times*. 'You're either upper class,
middle class or working class. Now I might be a multimillionaire,
but I'm still working class. Whereas America is classless. You're
either rich or you're poor.'

He liked the moral of Alfred P. Doolittle: that his life was
messed up once he sought admiration, and then money and
marriage. Similarly, the adulation The Who were shown at their
peak could have destroyed them. 'We fought against it,' said
Roger. We're a blue-collar people's band, and I'm glad we've
maintained it.'

With some 60 film and TV credits ranging from a BBC production of *The Beggar's Opera* to episodes of the popular TV series
Highlander, Roger is eminently capable of earning a living as an
actor and not many rocks stars can claim that. Thrown in at the
deep end in the movie *Tommy*, he was not given the chance to
make his mistakes in private. But by the time *My Fair Lady* came

along he felt confident enough in his ability to say: 'I've learned the craft and become a good actor.'

Ironically, perhaps the most-watched film starring Roger Daltrey is *The Kids Are Alright*, the remarkable documentary by Jeff Stein charting, with the aid of archive film material, the rise of The Who through their glory days. Recently released on DVD, *The Kids Are Alright* was originally premiered at the Cannes Film Festival on 13 May 1979, and was warmly lauded as the best rock 'n' roll documentary ever. Twenty-five years on, the updated version is not only a stunning visual record of the band at its best but also a valuable depiction of an important chapter in rock history.

As the DVD's notes reveal, Stein put up the idea for the film to Pete Townshend when they met at the New York premiere of the film version of *Tommy*. Stein had already met Pete years before when, as a 17-year-old American fan, he had put out a book of photographs of The Who's 1970 tour. He figured that new Who fans would be curious about the band's history and that a documentary of how they achieved their success would be of interest to them. Pete initially rejected the idea but later gave it his blessing. Everybody knew there would be an audience for such a movie when Stein saw the responses of all the members of The Who and their wives who had gathered to watch a 17-minute show reel he had put together of the band's US TV appearances.

'I've never seen such a reaction,' Stein is quoted as saying in the film notes. 'Townshend was on the floor banging his head. He and Moon were hysterical. Daltrey's wife was laughing so hard she knocked over the table in the screening room. Their reaction was unbelievable. They loved it. That's when they were really convinced that the movie was worth doing. It amused them, so they figured there must be an audience for it. They're always their harshest critics.'

CHAPTER ELEVEN

CLOSING RANKS

He was the most original drummer in rock. We could never replace him.

Roger Daltrey on the death of Keith Moon

On the night of 6 September 1978 one of the authors was a guest at a celebrity-packed party at the Peppermint Park restaurant in Upper St Martin's Lane, in London's West End, thrown by Paul McCartney to commemorate the birthday of Buddy Holly. The former Beatle, a huge Holly fan since boyhood, had recently acquired the publishing rights to the Texas rock pioneer's music catalogue, and to perpetuate Holly's memory and his music, Paul had declared the first week of September every year to be Buddy Holly Week.

The focal point of the 1978 Buddy Holly Week was the party at Peppermint Park, followed by a screening of the movie *The Buddy Holly Story*, starring Gary Busey. It was a relaxed, enjoyable occasion and among the guests were such luminaries as Eric Clapton and David Frost, as well as Keith Moon and his girlfriend, Annette Walter Lax.

Along with other guests, Keith and Annette left the party at around 11.30pm for the midnight screening at the nearby Dominion Theatre in Leicester Square. They had not long been settled in their seats when Keith decided to leave, followed swiftly by Annette. Next afternoon Annette found Keith dead in their bed, and an autopsy ruled that death had been caused by an overdose of Heminevrin, a sedative drug prescribed to fight alcoholism.

After a hedonistic adult life of terrible excess, Keith's death was not exactly unexpected but it nevertheless shook Roger, Pete and John to the core. They were all devastated. 'Everybody knew Moon was in trouble,' says Keith Altham, 'and everyone tried to help him. I know Roger tried very hard. But Moon was like a racing car running away downhill that could not be stopped. People would jump out and put a couple of chocks in front of the wheels, but Moon would jump out, kick them away and then carry on. It was very sad, but almost a foregone conclusion. Roger was very upset about it and so was Pete. Moon was their clown prince.'

Roger's immediate reaction to the news was one of terrible sadness rather than shock as he had seen Moon flirt with danger and abuse his body so often. 'It's the end of an era,' he said. 'He was the most original drummer in rock. We could never replace him because we've never met anyone like him. He was like a younger brother.'

At a subdued funeral service in the chapel of Golders Green Crematorium on 13 September 1978, there were wreaths and tributes from many of rock's top names, including Fleetwood Mac, Led Zeppelin, the Moody Blues, the Steve Gibbons Band, Stevie Winwood and Elton John. Roger comforted Keith's grieving mother and it was Roger's wreath that reminded everyone of Keith's colourful past. Yellow and white flowers were combined in the form of a television set with a champagne bottle thrown through it.

Shortly after Keith's death Roger attended a seance – not for the first time. It was something which didn't faze him since he had an aunt who was a medium and he had learned not to regard seances in candle-lit rooms as anything to be frightened of, strange or sin-ister.

Roger told the American TV host Robin Leach: 'We were going to break up the group. There didn't seem much point in going on without him. But then, at the seance, I heard Keith's spirit talking loud and clear. It was just like being on the phone with him in a not-too-far-away place. I told him we couldn't replace him if we had a hundred drummers.

'He told me there was only one choice to make. And I made it. The group decided we had to go on and Kenney Jones was the only choice to take his place. It was what Keith wanted. We followed his decision.' Roger concluded that for The Who to go on without Keith Moon was the only way to make sure his life hadn't been wasted. 'If we had let the band go then, it would have made two tragedies out of one.'

And, in a curious way, Keith's death galvanised the remaining members of The Who into closing ranks and going forward as a unit at a time when their disaffection with each other might have spelled the end. 'We were all fighting each other with real hate until that happened,' said Roger. 'But then, instead of calling it quits, we decided to go on. We learned to need each other instead of feuding.'

Kenney Jones, drummer in first the Small Faces and later the Faces with Rod Stewart as their lead singer, was well known to Roger, Pete and John. They had got to know Kenney when The Who and the Small Faces riotously toured Australia together in 1968. In truth, replacing Keith Moon was impossible since he was the most inventive drummer Roger had ever come across. But Kenney did a good job, though not always meeting with Roger's approval. In subsequent years Ringo Starr's son Zak Starkey took over.

Moon's death inevitably cast a dark shadow across the band's album *Who Are You*, released just three weeks earlier. In the saddest of ironies, Moon had been pictured on the cover sitting on a chair marked 'Not to be taken away'. Moon's death was the very saddest of postscripts to an album which had not been an easy undertaking for Roger. He had a series of disagreements with producer Glyn Johns over its production and the two of them had come to blows.

Over the next decade The Who announced farewell tours but still managed to re-form both on stage and in the recording studio. They were touring America when John Entwistle was found dead of a suspected heart attack in a Las Vegas hotel room on 27 June 2002, at the age of 57. He died in the company of a showgirl and with traces of cocaine in his bloodstream.

While Keith Moon's death had not been unexpected, Roger was not altogether surprised when the news of John's death reached him. 'John hadn't been healthy for a long time,' he said. 'I'm a big believer in alternative medicine and healthy living, and I can tell when someone looks ill. I saw it in John's pallor and his eyes. He lived hard and he took risks. Whenever I saw him in the last few years, I always made a habit of giving him a big hug before I left him. I was never sure I'd see him again.'

John's death occurred not long after he and the other members of The Who had come through a medical examination taken for insurance purposes for their upcoming US tour.

But as long as four years before John died, Roger had been concerned enough about John's health to speak to Pete Townshend about it, with the idea of their both approaching John and persuading him to have a check-up. Roger, with knowledge accumulated personally from his 30 years of alternative medicine treatment, had noticed John's grey pallor with very real anxiety and pointed it out to Pete. But in the end they decided to say nothing. 'We knew he had blood pressure problems,' said Roger, 'but no one thought to ask him to get his heart checked. But if we had, he would have told us to fuck off and mind our own business. Or just grunt and ask for another brandy.'

Roger was confident this would have been John's precise reaction because he had once raised the subject of cancer with the bass guitarist and John's head-in-the-sand response was that if he had any life-threatening illness then he simply didn't want to know about it.

Roger received the grim news over the phone from Pete. Having flown out to Los Angeles two weeks before the start of The Who's US tour, he was enjoying a leisurely lunch out with Heather when he got the chilling call. Pete said he needed to talk to Roger on his own.

Leaving Heather at the table, Roger went outside to hear Pete say: 'John died last night.' He instantly went numb. 'It was like being hit by a bat,' he remembers. 'I immediately drove over to Pete's hotel to be with him. I admit that I had wet eyes that night.'

John was laid to rest near his home at Stow-on-the-Wold in Gloucestershire. At the funeral, Roger poignantly wrote on his memorial card: 'It seems ridiculous to tell you to rest in peace, my friend, so Rave On.' It was, Roger explained, a fitting eulogy. 'You can't tell someone like John to rest in peace. It should be "Rest in Noise". I hope they've got earplugs up there – or down there because with him and Keith Moon there will be a bloody great rhythm section.' Roger was amused to find that some of John's dry and dark humour shone through even at the Ox's wake – the alcoholic drinks were free but soft drinks had to be paid for.

On a personal level, John's death was a hammer blow for Roger. He had come to regard John as a brother after so many years together. 'If anyone had come between us they would have had their heads ripped off,' he said. 'It's like a brotherly love, family embedded within you and we've been through so much together.' For Roger, John's willingness to tour had been a driving force to match his own ambitions about keeping The Who regularly on the road. If John had had his way, said Roger, The Who would have toured for all but two weeks of the year. 'He lived to play.'

Inevitably Roger and John had had their differences while living and working in such close proximity for some 40 years. Not least when Roger embarked on a 1994 solo tour celebrating Pete

Townshend's music, followed by a starry pay-per-view special involving John. The bass guitarist didn't entirely enjoy having Roger as his boss, a throwback to the days when the singer liked to lay down the law to the Detours.

There had been many a time when John had seriously considered quitting The Who, notably when he and Keith Moon arrived late for a gig at Newbury in 1966 to face the intense wrath of Roger and Pete. The furious greeting awaiting the tardy duo prompted Keith and John to spend many an hour plotting to form their own group from a collection of luminaries ranging from Jimmy Page to Steve Winwood and Jeff Beck. But John was ultimately aware that he needed the other members of The Who as much as they needed him.

As anchorman for The Who, John had tended to stay in the background on stage, content to let the more flamboyant and egotistical Keith, Pete and Roger fight it out for the limelight. He frequently wore black, was rarely picked out by a spotlight, and on television he was often invisible unless the camera flicked from Roger to Keith. But musically he was always solidly there, and when it came to the group's records Roger acknowledged that John's contribution was immense. Indeed, not long before his death, John had been voted Bass Player of the Millennium by his peers. And when Oasis were auditioning new bassists for their band, their acid test was to ask prospective candidates to play John's searing run from 'My Generation'. 'He was the best,' said Roger in tribute to John. 'As Bill Wyman said, he did for the bass guitar what Jimi Hendrix did for the lead guitar. He made the bass do things it was never meant to. Extraordinary.'

John's sudden death, coming just days before the start of The Who's American tour, inevitably threw the schedule into confusion. It called for some drastic rethinking. Predictably, the initial reaction from everyone involved was that the tour must be scrapped. Roger and Pete were in a no-win situation. If they went ahead with the tour, they would be accused of being insensitive. If they called it off, many thousands of fans who had bought tickets would be disappointed – the enduring pulling power of The Who had ensured that the 20,000-capacity Madison Square Garden in New York sold out in just 16 minutes.

For the 12 hours immediately after confirmation of John's death, the feeling prevailed that the tour could not possibly go on. But thereafter the question frequently asked was what John himself would have wanted. Would he have wanted it to be cancelled? The unanimous answer was that John, who loved touring, would have wished for the tour to go on, particularly as it was sold out and the band were responsible for literally thousands of people ranging from roadies, to promoters, to lighting companies to theatre staff. Roger himself was terribly torn, and the decision was ultimately left to Pete. 'Roger left entirely to me the decision as to whether or not to go on with the tour,' he wrote in the 'Pete's Diaries' section of www.petetownshend.com. 'I think [Roger] hoped in his heart it would not be over so suddenly.

'I don't feel I know for certain that John would have wanted us to go on. I simply believe we have a duty to go on, to ourselves, ticket buyers, staff, promoters, big and little people. I also have a duty to myself and my dependent family and friends.'

True to The Who's defiant nature, the decision was made to con-tinue and Roger and Pete ultimately agreed that soldiering on was the best way to honour their bandmate. Roger had no doubts in the end that it was absolutely the right decision. Death is part of life and life must go on, was Roger's view. 'We're very lucky to be alive,' he said. 'Life is precious, and we should enjoy it. We'd been with John 40-odd years and I shall miss him terribly. But I think we do owe it to our generation, who are this age, to show them that they're going to be losing friends more and more. We need to show the way by saying: "You don't give up, you carry on."'

Once the decision had been taken, the practicality of continuing was hastily solved, first by the postponement of two weekend dates and then by the immediate hiring of Pino Palladino, a bass guitarist much respected among rock's elite. Pino had played on dozens of records by artists such as Eric Clapton, Phil Collins and Rod Stewart, he was an experienced session and touring musician, and he had featured on Townshend albums and solo tours. Even so, it was deemed sensible to cut from the set most of the new material, the first fresh songs Pete had written for The Who for some 20 years.

Happily for Roger and Pete, there was also no question that the two of them could no longer call themselves The Who. After the equally sudden death of Keith Moon, the remaining three band members had agreed among themselves that if anything happened to one or other of them, the surviving members could continue to carry the name and play under the banner of The Who. Now, joining the two original Who members Pete and Roger for the tour were drummer Zak Starkey, a regular since 1996, Pete's brother Simon Townshend on rhythm guitar and backing vocals, and long-time keyboard accompanist John 'Rabbit' Bundrick.

The deep sense of the loss of John really sank in when Roger and Pete next got together for a rehearsal. It was a distressing moment when they ran through a number without the Ox for the very first time. Perversely, John Entwistle's death ensured the band's opening concert at the Hollywood Bowl on 1 July 2002 was probably the most intently observed and scrutinised Who gig since Kenney Jones had taken his seat on the drum stool as the replacement for Keith Moon in 1979. The Hollywood Bowl audience could not help but wonder how the band, in their grief and uncertainty, would fare both emotionally and musically, without Entwistle.

The embrace between Roger and Pete at the start of the show before a single note was played set the poignant tone for the evening, and Roger left no one in any doubt where everybody's thoughts lay when he declared: 'Tonight we play for John Entwistle. He was the true spirit of rock 'n' roll, and he lives on in all the music we play.'

Critics at the show noted there seemed to be an extra burst of energy about the opening salvo of 'I Can't Explain', 'Substitute' and 'Anyway Anyhow Anywhere' as if to stress the show must go on as well as reminding the capacity crowd of the power created by The Who in its halcyon days with John and Keith. Considering he had managed to fit in just two days of rehearsals playing bass on numbers he had never played before, Pino Palladino coped admirably with more than two hours of vintage Who material. Inevitably, all eyes and ears were on him from the outset and the crowd clearly warmed to him from the start. There was patent respect for Pino that he had stepped into the breach at such short notice and sympathy for him that he now found himself in the spotlight through the most tragic of circumstances. Pino won himself a special cheer for his stab at Entwistle's famously rollicking bass run in 'My Generation'.

Without being overambitious, Pino fitted in so well and the show progressed so smoothly that Pete found it necessary to stress that this was so much more than just another Who gig. Stepping to the front of the stage, he told the crowd: 'This is going to be very difficult,' he said. 'We understand. We're not pretending that nothing's happened.' Later Roger publicly thanked Pino by saying: 'He rescued us in the nick of time.' The concert ended with photographs of Entwistle flashed up on video screens to huge, sympathetic applause.

The immense emotional hurdle of that first concert without John safely negotiated, the relief for Pete and Roger was evident for all to see. 'As soon as we started playing it was like John was back,' said Roger. 'He's in that music, just like Keith Moon is. That really helped with the grieving.'

As the tour gathered pace, Roger was quick to praise Pino further. 'It was a stretch for him, because he hadn't played any of these songs before. But he's doing extremely well,' he said halfway through the tour. 'He's the perfect choice. He's one of the best session players in the world, and he could mimic John perfectly if that's what we wanted him to do, but we don't. He adds his own stuff to the songs and makes them different. And as soon as he starts playing, John exists within the music anyway – he's just intrinsically there.'

Naturally, Roger had to field questions from the press, who pointed out that a second member of The Who dying a drug-related death represented a terrible waste. Roger had a ready answer. 'Ask most blokes how they would like to go,' he told one inquisitor. 'On the seafront in Eastbourne in a bath chair or in Las Vegas after a line of coke and a good old bang with a hooker? If John could have planned it, he wouldn't have it different. If he'd had a postscript to his death it would have gone: 'Body to be embalmed, placed back in bed, guitars placed around room, door to be replaced with glass panel and scene to be used as Hard Rock Cafe exhibit.'

As the tour neared its end, Roger was at pains to stress that musically The Who had all the vitality it ever had, but now with a slightly different sound. In the main, reviews were favourable, but the odd one accusing The Who of merely going through the motions made him incandescent with anger. He begged to differ and insisted they had risen to the musical challenge. 'I'm never going through the fuckin' motions,' he raged in one interview. 'The shows have been incredible. I've never seen Townshend play guitar like this since, God, 1969. He's on fire. He's never been bad, but I'm talking stratospheric now.'

The tour ended on 28 September 2002 in Toronto. Ironically, it was at Toronto's Maple Leaf Gardens in 1982 that The Who played what they thought at the time was the last concert of a much-bal-lyhooed farewell tour. Now they were playing the final concert of a tour which had turned out very differently from how it was planned. It had been an emotional three months and neither Roger nor Pete was clear about exactly what would happen once they had fulfilled their concert commitments.

Roger did, however, emerge from the tour full of optimism. He was excited that Pete had started writing for The Who again after two decades and he rated much of the material as superb. 'I feel that an intellect the like of Pete Townshend had the potential to write perhaps his best work at this age,' he said. Of course, John was much missed, but the tour had proved that he and Pete were the nucleus of The Who. 'The Who has transcended us,' Roger said. 'It's bigger than us. We had an awful lot of young people on this tour, a whole new audience, and you think, this is bigger than us now. They're all in The Who. I equate the band to a box where one side has fallen off and it leaves us a great deal of space to experiment. I'm very optimistic. In some ways there are more opportunities now. I think we should take the challenge and ride with it.'

Soon Roger was telling a Radio Academy conference: 'I'm still angry about a lot of things. So many things we thought would get better when we were young have not. Pete is the one person who can articulate this and drag rock 'n' roll into old age. He is still writing great songs about things we all feel and can identify with. We owe it to our audience and the talent we were given to carry on.'

The first real tangible sign that Roger and Pete felt the future still held much for the band came on 4 May 2004, with the release of the first new material by The Who in 22 years – a Pete Townshend meditation on mortality called 'Old Red Wine'. It was written for John and inspired by John's love of expensive claret – and his penchant for often drinking it past its prime.

There has never been an easy relationship between Roger Daltrey and Pete Townshend. In the early days The Who was Roger's band but gradually the force of Townshend's towering talent and powerful personality turned it into his band. And control is not something that Roger lost lightly. Through the years since their early success the two leading members of the band somehow negotiated an uneasy truce. They didn't speak for months at a time in some difficult periods and Pete always found Roger's constant dream of The Who getting together again to tour slightly difficult to deal with.

But as soon as Pete was in trouble he found he had no firmer friend in the world than Roger. And trouble arrived in the most horrendous way for him in January 2003. An international police investigation into child pornography on the internet had a list of names and addresses of British subscribers and Pete Townshend was on it.

Like most of the rest of the nation, Roger heard the shock information on the television news. He was totally stunned, and struggled to take it in. He might have argued bitterly with Pete on musical matters but he knew his lifelong friend was as straight as a die. The implication of the news bulletin was painfully clear to millions of viewers. Living legend Pete Townshend, the genius behind one of the greatest rock bands of all time, was being accused of being a paedophile. In most people's book it was much worse than being called a murderer. Yet instinctively Roger knew that this was deeply unjust and very wrong. He would happily have bet his life that Pete Townshend was innocent and he was absolutely furious at the accusation.

It is at dark times like this that you find out exactly who your real friends are. And while certain former associates chose to keep their heads down and their names out of any potentially damaging publicity, Roger was determined to talk to Pete and give him his support as soon as possible. However, he was deeply frustrated by not being able to get through to him in person. He wanted to provide more than just a message on an answerphone. But, understandably, no one was answering Townshend's number, so Roger was reduced to leaving a message saying that he knew his friend was going through a dreadful ordeal right now and frankly suggesting he had obviously done something very stupid. But he pledged his unconditional support and assured his friend that he believed his version of events showed he was innocent.

Roger's first concern was for Pete's immediate family, his wife and children and his brothers, who were all shocked and upset by the horrific news. He tried to reassure them all that the truth would soon come out and the cloud of suspicion over his friend would pass. And so it did, but it was a desperately painful process. Townshend insisted it was purely for research purposes that he had used a credit card once to enter a site advertising child porn. Roger knew instantly that this was true. He knew Townshend's passion for helping people and was well aware of the work he had done for people who had suffered abuse of all kinds. He accepted that Townshend had done something 'naive and stupid' that had left him wide open to the foulest accusations and the sort of public humiliation he received in the police investigation.

Going instantly on the record, Roger stated: 'I've known Pete for the best part of my life, since I was 15. But if I thought there was any truth in this whole thing then no way would I defend him. But anyone who knows him knows the amount of work he has done in all areas of abuse in the last 35 years – from helping battered wives to all the work he has done in prisons.' And Roger was quick to back up his friend's formal statement that he had entered the inter-net site for research purposes. 'His statement is the truth,' he said. 'No way did he do it for criminal or salacious reasons. Quite the reverse. Two years ago he told me how angry he was at these sites and at the lack of action by the authorities who could control them. He has got a huge passion about the internet and how it is being abused.'

Roger sensibly pointed out that Townshend's very concern led him to believe that he needed to know exactly what he was talking about. But he went on to explain that it would have been easy for Townshend to lie or blame someone else, but instead he chose to tell the truth. 'And he gets pilloried,' he said. 'What they have done to him is appalling. They've pilloried a really, really, really good man. It's horrendous.'

In fact, Townshend even found himself appearing on a major BBC television documentary on 'Operation Ore', as the police investigation was known. Cameras followed police officers call-ing at the home of the bewildered-looking rock millionaire to take him in for humiliating questioning. After an exhaustive search of his computers Townshend was cautioned and put on the Sex Offenders' Register for five years. Roger, along with Townshend's family and friends, fumed at the unfairness of the whole experience. 'He did something incredibly naive, but he didn't do anything criminal, and to end up with any kind of a criminal record – even for a small period of time – is a dis-grace,' he said.

'He told the truth from the very beginning, from Day One. They went through his computers with an almost military preci-sion. None have been doctored. None have been tampered with. He never had one image. The whole thing was a scam. You have to understand, Pete is a Lennon character. Just like John he is a cre-ative artist who wears his heart on his sleeve and draws his own boundaries. The Establishment didn't like John for doing that and now they want to get Pete.'

CHAPTER TWELVE

FINALE

As long as Pete's there on guitar, and I'm there to sing the lead, then the sound's still there and you're going to have The Who. We're not going to give up now. We're going to keep playing until we're dead.

Roger Daltrey

There was a time in the late sixties when Roger's reluctance to join in the riotous shenanigans of The Who on tour earned him the nickname 'Auntie Daltrey'. According to Karl Green of Herman's Hermits, with whom The Who were touring, Roger won the moniker for 'being a bit of an old woman'. But if a defence was needed by the one-time tough from Shepherd's Bush for not always joining in with the mayhem and excesses instigated by Keith Moon, Roger could always point to the fact that he was for some years seriously on parole with The Who after his bust-up with Keith Moon had resulted in his being kicked out of the band.

Roger certainly had his wilder moments, like the time in Toronto in 1969 when he set alight roadie Bob Pridden's shoes after he had left them outside his hotel room to be cleaned. Within minutes the fire brigade had been called and furious hotel management then ordered The Who to leave and never to return. Amusingly for Roger, the prank was wrongly attributed by everyone to Keith Moon, who had become obsessed with cherry bomb firecrackers and regularly carried around a suitcase stuffed full of them for explosive purposes.

Generally, Roger's common sense, his determination to stay fit and healthy in order to give of his best on stage, and his wariness of drugs made him steer clear of the worst excesses of The Who as they criss-crossed America on tour. 'The only drug I could do was pot and I didn't used to do that very often because I couldn't sing on it – it dries your throat up,' Roger explained in Reel 2 of the updated DVD *The Kids Are Alright.* 'So it kept me away from it. I was very, very lucky.'

Besides, he pointed out, 'Someone had to be straight in the band because I was dealing with one alcoholic and probably drug addict in Keith, Pete was an alcoholic, and John was an alcoholic.' He admitted there were times when he would be the only sober one when everyone else was drunk as skunks and urging him to join them. 'I used to have fun in my own quiet way but with the band I used to always have to be the one otherwise it could all have gone pffft at any moment. It was like a bomb waiting to go off.'

In Montreal in 1973, Roger wisely retired to bed early as an after-show party thrown by MCA Records at the Bonaventure Hotel started to get out of hand. Moon, as usual was in the thick of it, having wreaked havoc and largely got away with it on previous tours. Quite aside from his bouts of destruction, he had once frightened the pants off Herman's Hermits' drummer Barry Whitham by putting the bloody head of a suckling pig in his bed, nailing chairs and tables to the ceiling of his hotel room and chilling a lobster on ice in his bathroom, conveniently using its claws to hold his room key.

Now, in Montreal, the outrageous mischief really began to kick off when Moon removed a painting from the wall, stomped the picture out of its frame, then replaced the empty frame around a painting of his own, created on the wall in tomato ketchup and mustard. Moon then stood back to admire his handiwork while seeking confirmation from others present that his abstract ketchup design was a much more agreeable work of art than the original painting. Soon other party-goers also set about redecorating the room Moon-style. The resulting make-over brought about complete devastation. Moon's *pièce de résistance* was to lift up a marble coffee table and, with the help of another guest, use it as a battering ram to smash a hole through the wall. Finally, the table was hurled through the window, followed swiftly by the television set, into the swimming pool 13 floors below.

The hotel management's response was to call in the Mounties. The Canadian Mounted Police are world famous for always getting their man. This time they got 16 of them. The Who's entire touring party, including tour manager Pete Rudge and Roger – who was thoroughly nonplussed at being woken in the early hours of the morning – were arrested and locked up for seven hours. The gravity of the proceedings as each was booked at the police station was lightened somewhat by Keith Moon, of course, who gave his name, leaned across the counter and said to the officer: 'I believe I booked a suite.'

Pete Rudge recalled in Tony Fletcher's biography *Dear Boy: The Life of Keith Moon* how, amazingly, he later saw Moon walking past the row of cells in his expensive silk smoking jacket, with a cigarette in a cigarette holder and a minion behind him carrying a bottle of champagne on a silver tray. Once the cell door had safely slammed shut with the elegantly attired Moon inside, the police also managed to see the funny side by piping The Who's music into everyone's cells for the rest of the night.

While much of the mayhem – and the hefty bills that followed to put right the damage The Who inflicted on their travels – could have been avoided, on stage, however, there could be strange, unexpected happenings which were unavoidable. On 16 May 1969, during the first of three shows at the Fillmore East, the famed rock venue on New York's Lower East Side, Roger was in the middle of singing 'Summertime Blues' when smoke started to filter into the back of the auditorium and alarmed members of the audience began leaving by the side doors. In fact, it was not the theatre that was on fire but Lion Groceries, an adjoining store. As promoter Bill Graham later explained: 'Someone had thrown a Molotov cocktail in the grocery store next door because the owner refused to pay protection money.'

The fans massed at the front of the theatre enjoying The Who and intently tuned in to the music were oblivious to the possible danger and Graham was about to make a formal announcement for evacuation of the building when plainclothes police officer Daniel Mulhearn of the Tactical Police Force ran on to the stage during 'Shakin' All Over' and grabbed the microphone from Roger. But before he could speak, a roadie rushed on to grab the man, and Roger, likewise unaware Mulhearn was a police officer public-spiritedly trying to stop the show and a possible conflagration, threw a punch at him while Pete aimed a kick. The fracas ended with Mulhearn leaping six feet off the stage. Keith and John, meanwhile, equally unaware of the intruder's identity, played on regardless while the 2,000-strong crowd cheered what they believed to be the ejection of some nutty killjoy. Finally, Bill Graham came on to announce the theatre was to be cleared, and the audience safely filed out into the street.

The police were none too pleased with the treatment of their undercover man and immediately descended on Loew's Midtown Hotel looking for Roger and Pete, but the band were holed up in Bill Graham's apartment. Next day, however, both Pete and Roger decided it would be for the best if they voluntarily presented themselves at the Ninth Precinct police station, where they were formally charged with assaulting a plainclothes police officer. It took a lengthy plea of mitigation by Kit Lambert and intervention on Roger and Pete's behalf by Bill Graham to persuade the police to release the two and remand them on bail. Roger and Pete were given permission to go just 45 minutes before their next gig was due to start. Six weeks later, at Manhattan's Supreme District Court, Pete was fined $75 on a reduced charge of harassment. The charges against Roger were summarily dismissed.

A year earlier Roger and the other members of The Who's touring party in Australia suffered the indignation of being escorted by security guards from a plane with their hands in the air, then left sitting for six hours in an aircraft hangar by the side of a runway to cool off.

This humiliation followed a fracas on the plane carrying The Who from Adelaide to Sydney at the end of a chaotic short tour of Australia in 1968. Also on the plane were Paul Jones, former singer with Manfred Mann, and The Who's rival Mod band the Small Faces, all of whom had been booked for a package tour called 'The Big Show', to bring a sample of Britain's beat boom to their Antipodean cousins.

The flare-up on the plane began when a stewardess spotted a member of Paul Jones's Aussie support band, the Questions, opening a bottle of beer which had been smuggled aboard. From that moment on she refused to serve coffee to anyone, and when angry words were exchanged between her and roadie Bob Pridden, she burst into tears and shot off to the captain's cabin to complain. An off-duty pilot also accused the groups of using obscene language and of being drunk. Soon the captain was informing tour manager Ron Blackmore that the plane would be landing at Melbourne so that they could all be arrested. At the city's Essendon airport they were duly escorted off the plane in humiliating fashion like criminals by State and Commonwealth police and held by airport security officers.

Right from the start of the tour things had not gone well. Arriving in Sydney after a gruelling 36-hour flight with stops at Cairo, Bombay, Karachi and Singapore, Roger and the rest were herded into a press conference which got off to a bad start when one of the Small Faces was asked if he was a drug addict. The reply amounted to two words, one of them a four-letter expletive, which immediately set the press against the entire group of musicians. It wasn't long before they were all being labelled in the newspapers as filthy, long-haired Pommie yobs.

Any hope that they might regain lost ground with the media by their performances onstage was lost when The Who discovered how outdated the PA systems were at the concert venues, some of which were little more than boxing rings under tin roofs with anti-quated Tannoy speakers. In Sydney The Who appeared on a revolving stage which needed several men to push it round. But the sheer weight of the equipment caused it to grind to a halt halfway, leaving a large section of the audience watching the group's backsides.

After Steve Marriott, frontman with the Small Faces, showed some aggression on stage and threatened 'to clip some bleedin' ears', he was pelted with coins for his troubles and The Who were also accused of using foul language. It prompted Mr R.W. Askin, the New South Wales premier, to call for tougher action by the police in order to 'protect certain standards of decency. Especially when young impressionable girls of 12 and 13 are present.' The impressionable 12- and 13-year-old girls at the gigs were, of course, going delirious screaming with excitement at Roger, Pete, Keith and John, even if local DJ Stan Rofe found The Who's destructive finale too much to take. It left him with a feeling of nausea, he said.

After the farcical aforementioned airport arrest, the by now not-so-merry band flew on to New Zealand, where, their reputation having preceded them, an equally hostile Kiwi press awaited their arrival. In Wellington Roger and the others booked into the high-rise Waterloo Hotel, where the first item on the schedule was a party to celebrate Steve Marriott's twenty-first birthday. Generously, the Small Faces' record company, EMI, presented Steve with the gift of a portable record player and several records. As the booze flowed and the party became more raucous, unfortu-nately one of the records skipped a groove and in frustration Steve slammed his fist down so hard on the lid that it broke. Now the record player was useless, Steve decided the best thing to do was to chuck it away – out of the window. It soared over the balcony and landed on the hotel forecourt, breaking into smithereens

As Steve later publicly admitted, indulging in such an act of wanton vandalism in front of Keith Moon was perhaps not the best idea. It was the signal a pent-up Moon had been waiting for and all hell broke loose. By the time Moon had finished leading the party-goers in acts of frenzied destruction, the room was left trashed and bare. A shocked Steve, who had never seen Moon at his room-wrecking worst, later recounted: 'Before you knew it there were chairs, TVs, settees, everything was over the balcony and through the windows – mirrors everything, the whole deal. All the French doors were gone, every window, there's nothing in the room because it's all on the pavement.'

When the hotel launched an investigation, Marriott spun the unlikely story that intruders had broken into his room and destroyed it. And, quite incredibly, the hotel somehow believed him and set about redecorating the room and replacing the furniture. It was a comfort to Roger and the others that there would be no fat bill to pay for the destruction.

Just as incredibly, EMI decided to replace Steve's record player with an upgraded, much better model – a big stereo system with vast speakers, gleaming turntable and separate amp. Everyone agreed it would pump out music at a fantastic volume at the end-of-tour party everyone was looking forward to after the farewell shows by The Who and the Small Faces at Wellington's town hall.

After the bands had played their last gig, everyone assembled in Steve's refurbished room again for the end-of-tour party. When Keith Moon arrived, he took one look at Steve's super de luxe, state-of-the-art record player and promptly threw it out of the window. Steve was aghast, but it was too late. As before, it was the signal for utter devastation to begin. Putting the seal on a sequence of astonishing events, when the police were called to calm everyone down, they did nothing of the sort. They joined in. 'We had the police drunk, listening to Booker T, wearing their helmets and smashing the place up,' Steve recalled incredulously.

Once again the room was totally wrecked, but the hotel management were smarter the second time around and the tour ended with a huge bill for the damage caused and armed security guards posted outside Steve's door.

On 1 February The Who flew out of New Zealand with vitriol pouring from the pages of the Kiwi tabloid *The Truth*. The newspaper reported in a story entitled 'Paul Rodgers Boos The Who': 'They're the scruffiest bunch of Poms that ever milked money from this country's kids … they took nearly 8,000 teenagers for $2.60 to $3.60 each. All the kids got for their money was an ear-splitting cacophony of electronic sounds that was neither musical nor funny… They did more harm to the British image than Harold Wilson or Edward Heath could do in ten years. I'm ashamed to come from the same country as these unwashed, foul-mouthed, booze-swilling no-hopers. Britain can have them.'

Roger Daltrey has always had mixed feelings about touring with The Who. 'The road, to me, has always been a love-hate relationship,' he explained recently. 'I loathe it 22 hours of the day. But those other two hours in front of the audience make it all worthwhile.'

At the age of 60, it's understandable that the city-bred rock star prefers to indulge his lifelong rural fantasies, spending the majority of his hours on his Sussex farm, where he raises beef cattle and worms. The second, he notes, are useful for both fishing and, in an experimental way, organic waste disposal. It's a world away from 'the peroxide Teddy boy, the sort of person you'd prefer to stay on the other side of the street from', as Entwistle once described the youthful Roger. The rebellious swaggering teenager who made good through rock 'n' roll is concerned enough to operate his farm at a loss because, he says, the men who run it represent 'centuries and centuries of knowledge about how things work. If we lose that knowledge, it's not like a machine you can flip back on.' A born survivor, Roger insisted on teaching his son how to shoot a rabbit, skin it, cook it and eat it. 'We're going to need to know that stuff,' he says. 'And it will happen, whether it's in our lifetime or his or his kids'.'

Roger and the band said a false farewell in 1983, then in 1989 a goodbye which also proved to be a seriously premature swansong. The Who may have been inactive for long periods, but they have never gone away. Now, incredibly, 40 years after they played their first gigs in Shepherd's Bush dance halls, Roger and Pete see no reason why they should bring the curtain down on The Who. Especially when their teaming up together can raise money for the Teenage Cancer Trust. Last year the prestigious American magazine *Time* officially recognised Roger's fund-raising and awareness campaign by including him in their inaugural list of European Heroes.

Keith Moon and John Entwistle were, of course, essential ingredients of The Who, but few would quibble when Roger points out that he and Pete Townshend were always the driving force behind the band, the real nucleus. 'As long as Pete's there on guitar, and I'm there to sing the lead, then the sound's still there and you're going to have The Who,' he declares. 'We're not going to give up now. We're going to keep playing until we're dead.'

Those closest to Roger do not disbelieve him, nor aim to dissuade him. 'Roger will go on as long as possible,' says Keith Altham. 'He gets tremendous satisfaction raising money for his cancer charity. He's a guy really enjoying putting something back.

'How will he be remembered? The Who were the greatest rock band that ever lived, and he was the singer in that band. That's one hell of an accolade. To me, musically they were the best band of the lot, better than the Rolling Stones, the Beach Boys, the Doors. Nothing compared to The Who live when they were on song. I'll never forget The Who playing at Charlton Football Club in the rain. They blew me away – and I was their PR. I was quite blasé about them, but I stood there in total awe. Townshend and Daltrey together on stage were almost balletic although neither were really great dancers – Roger was more of a marcher. But you look at them together as a combination and they were somehow united in their movements and were amazing to watch.

'As a singer I don't think Roger ever modelled himself on anyone. He's unique. When he became a singer, he just learned how to project and improve. He doesn't sound like anyone else, which probably makes for a good rock star. I think he'll also be remembered as a reasonably successful actor, for some solo singles, and for his movies that have done quite well. And I think he'll be remembered as a successful showbiz entity, for want of a better cliché.'

After four decades of rows, arguments and extraordinary achievements together, it is ironic that the two most volatile members of The Who should be the ones to survive and continue to carry the flag. The truth is that they needed each other and have respect for each other, a healthy mutual regard not aired often enough in public. 'Pete's are classic songs,' Roger happily admitted recently. 'When I look at the writers in the last century of rock 'n' roll, I have to put Townshend probably at number one. Not only did he lyrically write rock 'n' roll, he musically moved it.'

There was a genuine admiration expressed when Roger told one of the authors: 'The Who's music will go on long after I'm gone and Pete's gone. I really believe that. I get bored singing stuff other than Townshend's lyrics. When you're singing what's written, you have to believe it so it puts you through all kinds of turmoil. It's like being an actor and finding a part, it's incredibly challenging. Most music to me apart from that is boring. It's all too easy. I've always been an incredible fan of Pete's writing.' In 1994 Roger showed his allegiance when he assembled his own orchestra, signed up notable rock legends David Sanborn and Linda Perry and went on the road on a tour called 'A Celebration: The Music of Pete Townshend and The Who'.

Roger genuinely believes Pete's music is to be celebrated. 'It troubles me,' he says, 'that because pop is so fickle and ever-changing, that Pete's kind of quality of writing can get lost. It's tragic, although it's not so bad in America because they've got classic rock radio stations that just play old bands, so we're all right. But in England, all you ever hear is "My Generation" or "Substitute". You never hear the really good stuff from *Quadrophenia*. Music of that quality wasn't pop but a pop content which meant that you get hooked by it very quickly but it was like a very rich cake at the end of a very good meal. The way that the music was structured, the chords Townshend used to play was an acquired taste but, I think, wonderful. How the soundtrack of *Tommy* didn't win best movie soundtrack of the year, for example, I don't know. That must have been the best music in a film, surely.'

For his part, Pete is aware of the life Roger breathed into his songs to turn them from rawest musical demo doodles into worldwide hits. 'Pete always used to say he wrote his best songs for me through a third person,' Roger explains. 'And I think I was just confused, angry, bull-headed, but also a great actor and performed those songs as well as he could ever have imagined. I changed them from being the wimpy songs he envisioned that they were when he sang them.

'I just changed the songs radically. I think if you listen to the original demos, the way I sang the songs and the notes I put on them were totally different.

'I think I made the songs more touchable to more people. And that was The Who.'

CHAPTER THIRTEEN

TEENAGE WASTELAND

*For want of a better way of putting it, she had a light in
her eyes which for me was her spirit. I really reached
through to her spirit. It was incredible.*

Roger Daltrey, on the last time he saw his
dying sister Carol in hospital

The deaths of Keith Moon and then John Entwistle were, of
course, the bitterest of blows for Roger. He had lost friends before,
like Rolling Stone Brian Jones, Jimi Hendrix and Jim Morrison,
but Keith and John were two friends who had each played such a
major part in shaping his life. Together as bandmates they had
travelled all over the world, they had shared good times and bad,
fights and friendship, failure and success, poverty and wealth, crit-
icism and acclaim. Roger has always been quick to acknowledge
the vital individual contributions of each, which helped make The
Who the greatest band in the world.

But long before John Entwistle passed away, Roger's attitude to
death – notably learning not to be frightened of it – had been
shaped by tragedies and sadness even closer to home. First his
youngest sister, Carol, died at the tragically young age of 32 after a
two-year fight against breast cancer. Then, in a cruel twist of fate,
his parents, Harry and Irene, whom he witnessed suffering such

severe distress while closely watching and supporting Carol throughout her pain and suffering, both died from lung cancer. It was seeing how devastated his parents were by their daughter's death that led Roger to throw his energies, time and money behind the Teenage Cancer Trust. The charity creates specialist hospital units for British teenagers and young adults with cancer, leukaemia, Hodgkin's and related diseases, and creates a homely environment for them.

Roger seldom talks about Carol's death. He misses her desperately, and those closest to him note that tears unashamedly well up in his eyes on the very rare occasions he chooses to put into words the deep sadness he felt for Carol, the pain and ordeal she went through, and the distress it caused his entire family.

Carol's brave fight against breast cancer ended while Roger was away with The Who in 1983 on what was intended to be the band's final world tour. But he does not feel bad about not being at Carol's side when she passed away. That is much too negative, he says, to dwell on for the rest of his life. And, in any case, he knows that on his last hospital visit to Carol he made a remarkable spiritual connection with his sister which both understood was a last goodbye, for she knew he was off on a long tour. Both knew they would not see each other again.

The last time he saw her, brother and sister shared an incredible spiritual moment, with Roger standing beside Carol's hospital bed at a time when she was feeling terrible after an operation to remove her pituitary gland. Roger had seen her go through first the fear when she was diagnosed with cancer, then the eventual acceptance of the disease as it spread. Throughout her ordeal he had frequently talked to her about how the spirit survives, that death was the opening of another door. Now, with Carol at her lowest physical ebb, Roger looked deep into her eyes, she looked right back at him, and he knew that she understood.

In a moment of remarkable emotional togetherness, he saw that she knew she was dying, that she had come to terms with it with

his help. 'She was absolutely at one with herself,' he told one con-
fidante. 'For want of a better way of putting it, she had a light in
her eyes which for me was her spirit. I really reached through to her
spirit. It was incredible. I knew at the end she had enough strength
to be fine, she could cope, and since then I have never been afraid,
death doesn't worry me at all.'

While Carol was desperately ill Roger saw at first hand not just
her own suffering but the effect it had on those closest to her as she
was moved from hospital to hospital. He saw for himself the limitations of the National Health Service when it came to cancer
treatment. It made him aware of the need to change the system for
treating cancer patients and helping their families. He remembers
how he and his parents were allowed to see Carol only during vis-
iting hours. If, for some reason, they were unable to arrive at the
hospital at the appointed hour, they were not permitted to see her.
Roger resented this lack of compassion and was disturbed to find
that Carol was moved from hospital to hospital rather than
remaining in one hospital with the necessary equipment to cope.
He saw how heavily her ordeal weighed on Harry and Irene, particularly his mother. He noted also the effect on Carol's husband
and their two small children. They were all devastated by her illness
and death. 'It's not only the patients who are victims, but the families too,' he says.

When Roger was a boy, he and his sisters took up smoking cigarettes, just as their parents did. Harry and Irene were both almost
chain-smokers at a time when smoking was considered smart. In
those days many a Hollywood hero and heroine projected what
was perceived as a cool aura by lighting up on the silver screen, and
it was a time when there was minimal research into the possibly
harmful effects of tobacco smoking. The teenagers of the 1950s
were not discouraged from smoking, and Roger and his sisters followed the trend.

Roger eventually gave up cigarettes in the 1970s but remembers
his father smoking at least 40 a day. Ultimately, lung cancer

claimed Harry's life, and Irene, who had smoked around 30 a day all her adult life, died from the same disease. 'Mercifully for my mum, anyway, it was very quick,' he says. 'She went in five or six weeks, which can happen with old people.'

The Who have always done more than their fair share for charity – including playing Live Aid and the Concert for New York after the atrocities of 9/11. Roger's involvement with the TCT (Teenage Cancer Trust) began when he consulted Dr Adrian Whiteson, the noted sports-injury doctor, about injuries he had accumulated through years of touring. Dr Whiteson had set up the TCT some 12 years earlier and from him Roger learned that one in 330 boys and one in 440 girls get cancer in their teenage years, but there was virtually no proper provision for their care. Roger soon offered to help him raise some money towards the £25 million Dr Whiteson was aiming for to build the specialist units required.

Roger knew The Who were capable of sizeable fund raising because the band had just done so in America for the singer-song-writer Neil Young in aid of Down's Syndrome children. Getting the band back together specifically for concerts for the TCT was the obvious next step.

Now, thanks to a series of concerts, The Who's donation of £2 million has led to the establishment of six teenage cancer units in NHS hospitals in London, Leeds, Manchester, Newcastle and Birmingham. The target is 20 units, to enable every teenager with cancer in Britain to have access to such care.

Driving Roger on was his discovery that teenagers with cancer suffer discrimination at the hands of the NHS. He saw that they are classed either as an adult or a child and that in both cases their needs tend to get overlooked. If they are 16 they are treated as adults and put into adult wards with people who are dying, some of whom are very old. If they are 15 they are likely to find them-selves in a children's paediatric ward among small babies. Neither classification, he argues, helps an adolescent coping not only with puberty but a potentially terminal disease for which the treatments are often as painful as the disease itself.

'Imagine being 15, being told you've got bone cancer and you've got to have your leg amputated and you're there with babies crying,' he says. 'Or you could be 16 and in with old people dying. The psychological damage of either is horrendous.'

By staging a series of charity concerts featuring not just The Who but top groups like Coldplay, Roger has not only been raising funds for the Teenage Cancer Trust but also highlighting the problem. 'It is my mission, through these shows, to end this prejudice,' he says. 'Without teenagers there would be no pop industry and it is about time they are recognised by the NHS as the distinct group of people that they are. There have to be special units attached to hospitals, and families have to be provided for. My sister left two tiny children behind, who are now grown-up and doing fine,' he says. 'But it was awful for them when she was being moved from hospital to hospital, and terrible to be left without a mother from such a young age.'

In raising money to set up the hospital units especially designated for teenagers, Roger's reward is seeing that patients are allowed some dignity and parents can be with their teenage sons and daughters during their treatments and recovery, and even at the end if they die. Since the establishment of the TCT's hospital units, figures show a 15% improvement in recovery rates on the same treatment.

'We try to make it less like a hospital, more somewhere they almost look forward to going to,' Roger says of the units. 'It saves lives and helps parents, brothers and sisters as well. They feel so helpless. My parents buried my sister when she was young – just 32 – and they never really recovered.'

It's a sad fact that many of the teenagers in the special units do not survive. But part of Roger's campaign is to address the problems of those who do, to help them to live outside the units. He has seen for himself on visits to the wards how vulnerable they are while coping with the loss of their looks due to treatment, or facing a variety of difficulties such as obtaining a mortgage or health insurance.

'We must start trying to address these things honestly and not politically,' says Roger, who makes regular supportive visits to teenagers in the units. 'I feel Carol with me when I'm with these kids,' he says. 'Human life is not forever so there has to be something deeper. We should all try to cultivate that deeper part.'

Roger's commitment to the Teenage Cancer Trust is total. 'Once I get my teeth into something I never give up,' he says. 'Especially when I believe something's right.' It's the same stubborn, big-hearted drive which prompted him, along with other members of The Who, to show their public support for Rolling Stones Mick Jagger and Keith Richards when they were briefly jailed for drug possession after a notorious trial in 1967.

Roger was so horrified they had been imprisoned that he rallied Pete and Keith – John Entwistle was on his honeymoon – into making a stand on behalf of the incarcerated duo. The day after the 'Glimmer Twins' had been sentenced, the three Who members went into a recording studio to record a rush-released single consisting of two Stones songs, 'The Last Time' and 'Under My Thumb', with Pete filling in for John on bass. Within two days of Jagger and Richards being led to the cells, the record was out and got to number 44 in the charts in Britain.

Roger's plan was to keep recording Rolling Stones songs every week in protest until their two rock pals were released from prison. His idea was that Jagger and Richards might have been shut away in jail but there was no way the authorities were going to shut their music up. In the event, The Who's planned campaign was cut short when the pair were quickly set free.

EPILOGUE

Ladies and gentlemen, a nice little band from Shepherd's Bush ... the 'Oo!
MC Jeff Dexter introducing The Who to the 600,000-strong crowd at the Isle of Wight Festival on Sunday, 30 August 1970

Although Roger and his bandmates didn't fully realise it at the time, the weekend in June 1967 when Monterey staged the very first of the great outdoor pop music festivals was a high point in the history of pop music.

The Who had joined an incredible line-up of talent which included Jimi Hendrix, Janis Joplin, the Byrds, Otis Redding, the Animals, Canned Heat, Simon and Garfunkel, Ravi Shankar, Hugh Masekela, Buffalo Springfield, Laura Nyro, Electric Flag, the Paul Butterfield Blues Band, Quicksilver Messenger Service, the Blues Project, Country Joe and the Fish, the Mamas & the Papas, Booker T & the MGs and the Association.

And, as Clive Davis, then newly appointed chief recording executive of Columbia Records, observed after attending the three-day event: 'It was the first time that artists could just come up on stage in an endless stream and play for thousands of young people.'

The Who's electrifying performance at Monterey cemented their

growing reputation at the time and subsequently won them invita-
tions to Woodstock in 1969 and then to the Isle of Wight festival
that same year and the next.

But back in 1970, when Roger stepped out of the helicopter
transporting The Who to the Isle of Wight festival site at East
Aston Farm, near Freshwater, he cannot have imagined that he
would return 34 years later at the age of 60 to sing classic Who
numbers to a whole new generation of pop fans.

Among the line-up that The Who joined in 1970 were Bob
Dylan, Joan Baez, Richie Havens and Joni Mitchell, whose set was
interrupted by a man jumping on stage and shouting: 'This is just
a hippie concentration camp' – which prompted Joni to burst into
tears.

The 1970 festival marked the last-ever performance by Jimi
Hendrix – he was to die in a London flat three weeks later from
asphyxiation due to inhalation of his own vomit. It was also the last
live appearance in England by another tragic rock figure, Jim
Morrison, lead singer with the Doors, who was to meet an
untimely death in Paris from a heart attack less than a year later.
But it is The Who's much-lauded two-hour set that is still best
remembered by those who were at the festival.

The band didn't take the stage until around 2am on Sunday, 30
August 1970, because others had overrun, and by then an estimated 600,000 fans had gathered, believed to be The Who's largest
audience. When Roger launched into Tommy's 'See Me, Feel Me'
refrain, 25,000-watt spotlights operated from their own generator
at the back of the stage bathed the exhilarated crowd in brilliant
light and attracted every moth on the Isle of Wight in the process.
The band's performance ended at around five in the morning with
the then trademark smashing of instruments.

The winged army fluttering in the spotlights like darting ani-
mated snowflakes over acre after acre of the massed ranks of fans
was better than any special effect, remembers tour manager John

Wolff. Better even, he thought, than the godsend of the fortu-itously timed sunrise at Woodstock, which occurred as if by command at the same moment in the same song.

Ray Manzarek from the Doors, who watched the band's now legendary set from the side of the stage, said: 'The Who were just amazing. They seemed to be on for two hours or more, and they would have just kept on playing but Pete Townshend's guitar broke. I remember he came off stage furious that he couldn't keep playing.'

Roger is not one for looking back. He likes to live for the day and surprise himself by what he can achieve today. But returning to play the Isle of Wight in 2004 inevitably brought back a host of memories – and notable contrasts. Back in 1970 bad weather marred the August festival. In 2004 the many thousands of fans who flocked to Newport's Seaclose Park basked in glorious mid-June sunshine. In 1970 Roger remembered, he shared bottles of Southern Comfort with Jim Morrison while seated around a big campfire lit by The Who's roadies to stave off the cold of the crisp, almost autumnal night air. By 2004 Roger's preferred tipple was healthy green tea.

Thirty-four years earlier Roger was a rock god, his shoulder-length hair a mass of curls, the crucifix around his neck bouncing off his bare, glistening chest. Now he was soberly dressed, fuller in the face, still an icon but one who happily admitted he was a regu-lar Radio 4 listener, a man who still preferred to write and post letters rather than wrestle with the complexities of computers and e-mails, and a grandfather to eight grandchildren.

And this time, of course, there was no Keith Moon to drop raw eggs into everyone's drinks for a lark, as he had done in 1970, and no John Entwistle offering snippets of dark humour. On stage in their place were Zak Starkey – who had been The Who's preferred drummer for the best part of a decade and was talented enough to be the choice of Noel and Liam Gallagher to play with Oasis at the Glastonbury festival just a few weeks later – and veteran session bassist Pino Palladino, by now an integral musical component after stepping into the breach so manfully after John Entwistle died.

Many hundreds of long-time Who fans trekked to the Isle of Wight to cheer Roger and Pete once more and to relive memories of seeing The Who at their peak. Their presence was enough to prompt Roger into speaking of his nerves at being asked to live up to the fans' expectations. 'You always doubt your ability,' he confessed, 'because you never really succeed in doing what you want to do, and that's why I keep coming back.'

For younger members of the audience, like 23-year-old Karen Dunn from Portsmouth, seeing The Who was a revelation. 'I really didn't know a lot about them and certainly didn't know what to expect,' she said. 'But they were terrific – they played with such passion and energy and sheer professionalism that you couldn't fail to be moved by them.'

For the critics too, The Who's return was an unqualified success. 'Roger Daltrey and Pete Townshend of The Who delivered a masterclass in mind-crushingly intense power rock,' reported the *Daily Telegraph*. 'Back in 1970, The Who had hoped that they would die before they got old. It's to our immeasurable benefit that not all of them have done so,' wrote Dan Silver in *The Times*. The presence at the Isle of Wight festival of critics from such august publications as these two papers was a sign that since 1970 times had indeed been a-changing.

Dan Silver also noted that The Who performed with plenty of exuberance and with an energy and enthusiasm that belied their years. 'It helps, of course,' he wrote, 'that they have one of rock's finest back catalogues this side of the Beatles, and "[I] Can't Explain", "Substitute" and "Who Are You?" got the band's set off to a flyer. Pete Townshend, dressed in sober black suit and T-shirt, may not be as freewheeling as in his youth, but his guitar playing has lost none of its pyrotechnic power, and Roger Daltrey's voice remains as rich and redolent as it ever was. Furthermore, they seemed to enjoy their set as much as their fans, Townshend lightheartedly acknowledging the passing of time with frequent references to the band's last performance here in 1970. "Most of you," he told the crowd, "were probably … started here.'"

Roger recognises that music simply isn't as important to young people's lives today as it was when he was a teenager. Then, it was all he had, and having discovered it and the ability to make it, he was never going to let go. Nor will he let it go now. He sometimes asks whether Pete ever had quite the same passion for and dedication to The Who as he has. 'You can't take me away from The Who,' he stressed recently. 'I drop everything for the band. I'm unconditionally a Who man.' Returning to the Isle of Wight after so many years is ample proof of that. It could have been a disaster.

As far as Roger is concerned, The Who must go on because he firmly believes their music will be ranked in history alongside Mozart's and Handel's and that no one can play it better than The Who. So while he and Pete are still capable, he intends for The Who to survive. And he predicts that the best of Pete's atomic chords, as he calls them, are still to come.

ALBUMS BY The Who

(THE WHO SINGS) MY GENERATION
December 1965

Side One:
Out in the Street
I Don't Mind
The Good's Gone
La-La-La-Lies
Much too Much
My Generation

Side Two:
The Kids Are Alright
Please Please Please
It's Not True
I'm a Man
It's a Legal Matter
The Ox

A QUICK ONE
December 1966

Side One:
Run Run Run
Boris the Spider
I Need You
Whiskey Man

Heatwave
Cobwebs and Strange

Side Two:
Don't Look Away
See My Way
So Sad About Us
A Quick One While He's Away

THE WHO SELL OUT
November 1967

Side One:
Armenia City in the Sky
Heinz Baked Beans
Mary Anne with the Shaky Hand
Odorono
Tattoo
Our Love Was, Is
I Can See for Miles

Side Two:
I Can't Reach You
Medac
Relax
Silas Stingy
Sunrise
Rael, 1 and 2

MAGIC BUS – THE WHO ON TOUR
1968

Side One:
Disguises
Run Run Run
Dr Jekyll and Mr Hyde

I Can't Reach You
Our Love Was
Call Me Lightning

Side Two:
Magic Bus
Someone's Coming
Doctor, Doctor
Bucket T
Pictures of Lily

DIRECT HITS
November 1968

Side One:
Bucket T
I'm a Boy
Pictures of Lily
Doctor, Doctor
I Can See for Miles
Substitute

Side Two:
Happy Jack
The Last Time
In the City
Call Me Lightning
Mary Anne with the Shaky Hand
Dogs

TOMMY (double)
May 1969

Side One:
Overture
It's a Boy

1921
Amazing Journey
Sparks
Eyesight to the Blind (The Hawker)

Side Two:
Christmas
Cousin Kevin
The Acid Queen
Underture

Side Three:
Do You Think It's Alright?
Fiddle About
Pinball Wizard
There's a Doctor
Go to the Mirror!
Tommy Can You Hear Me
Smash the Mirror
Sensation

Side Four:
Miracle Cure
Sally Simpson
I'm Free
Welcome
Tommy's Holiday Camp
We're Not Gonna Take It

THE HOUSE THAT TRACK BUILT
June 1969
Sampler of Track artists with three tracks by The Who.

Side One:
1. Magic Bus
4. Young Man's Blues

Side Two:
13. A Quick One While He's Away

LIVE AT LEEDS
May 1970

Side One:
Young Man Blues
Substitute
Summertime Blues
Shakin' All Over

Side Two:
My Generation
Magic Bus

WHO'S NEXT
August 1971

Side One:
Baba O'Riley
Bargain
Love Ain't for Keeping
My Wife
The Song Is Over

Side Two:
Getting in Tune
Going Mobile
Behind Blue Eyes
Won't Get Fooled Again

MEATY BEATY BIG AND BOUNCY
November 1971

Side One:
I Can't Explain

The Kids Are Alright
Happy Jack
I Can See for Miles
Pictures of Lily
My Generation
The Seeker

Side Two:
Anyway Anyhow Anywhere
Pinball Wizard
A Legal Matter
Boris the Spider
Magic Bus
Substitute
I'm a Boy

QUADROPHENIA (double)
October 1973

Side One:
I Am the Sea
The Real Me
Quadrophenia
Cut My Hair
The Punk Meets the Godfather

Side Two:
I'm One
The Dirty Jobs
Helpless Dancer
Is It in My Head
I've Had Enough

Side Three:
5.15
Sea and Sand

Drowned
Bell Boy

Side Four:
Doctor Jimmy
The Rock
Love Reign O'er Me

ODDS & SODS
October 1974

Side One:
Postcard
Now I'm a Farmer
Put the Money Down
Little Billy
Too Much of Anything
Glow Girl

Side Two:
Pure and Easy
Faith in Something Bigger
I'm the Face
Naked Eye
Long Live Rock

THE WHO BY NUMBERS
October 1975

Side One:
Slip Kid
However Much I Booze
Squeeze Box
Dreaming from the Waist
Imagine a Man

Side Two:
Success Story
They Are All in Love
Blue, Red and Grey
How Many Friends
In a Hand or a Face

THE STORY OF THE WHO (double)
September 1976

Side One:
Magic Bus
Substitute
Boris the Spider
Run Run Run
I'm a Boy
Heatwave
My Generation

Side Two:
Pictures of Lily
Happy Jack
The Seeker
I Can See for Miles
Bargain
Squeeze Box

Side Three:
Amazing Journey
The Acid Queen
Do You Think It's Alright?
Fiddle About
Pinball Wizard
I'm Free
Tommy's Holiday Camp

We're Not Going to Take It
Summertime Blues

Side Four:
Baba O'Riley
Behind Blue Eyes
Slip Kid
Won't Get Fooled Again

WHO ARE YOU
August 1978

Side One:
New Song
Had Enough
905
Sister Disco
Music Must Change

Side Two:
Trick of the Light
Guitar and Pen
Love is Coming Down
Who Are You

THE KIDS ARE ALRIGHT (double)
June 1979

Side One:
My Generation
I Can't Explain
Happy Jack
I Can See for Miles
Magic Bus
Long Live Rock

Side Two:
Anyway Anyhow Anywhere
Young Man (Blues)
My Wife
Baba O'Riley

Side Three:
A Quick One While He's Away
Tommy Can You Hear Me
Sparks
Pinball Wizard
See Me, Feel Me

Side Four:
Join Together
Road Runner
My Generation Blues
Won't Get Fooled Again

FACE DANCES
March 1981

Side One:
You Better You Bet
Don't Let Go the Coat
Cache Cache
The Quiet One
Did You Steal My Money

Side Two:
How Can You Do It Alone
Daily Records
You
Another Tricky Day

IT'S HARD
September 1982

Athena
It's Your Turn
Cooks County
It's Hard
Dangerous
Eminence Front
I've Known No War
One Life's Enough
One at a Time
Why Did I Fall for That
A Man Is a Man
Cry If You Want

THE WHO LIVE AT THE ISLE OF WIGHT FESTIVAL 1970
October 1996

Disc 1:
Heaven and Hell
I Can't Explain
Young Man's Blues
I Don't Even Know Myself
Water
Overture
It's A Boy
1921
Amazing Journey
Sparks
Eyesight to the Blind (The Hawker)
Christmas

Disc 2:
The Acid Queen
Pinball Wizard

Do You Think It's Alright
Fiddle About
Tommy Can You Hear Me
There's A Doctor
Go to the Mirror!
Smash the Mirror
Miracle Cure
I'm Free
Tommy's Holiday Camp
We're Not Gonna Take It
Summertime Blues
Shakin' All Over
Substitute
My Generation
Naked Eye
Magic Bus

THE WHO LIVE AT THE ROYAL ALBERT HALL
July 2003

Recording of live show in aid of the Teenage Cancer Trust

EP'S BY THE WHO

READY STEADY WHO!
December 1966

Side One:
Batman
Bucket T
Barbara Ann

Side Two:
Disguises
Circles

TOMMY
1970

Side One:
Overture from *Tommy*
Christmas

Side Two:
I'm Free
See Me, Feel Me

SINGLES BY THE WHO

I'm the Face (as the High Numbers) – July 1964
I Can't Explain – January 1965
Anyway Anyhow Anywhere – May 1965
My Generation – November 1965
Substitute – March 1966
A Legal Matter – March 1966
I'm a Boy – August 1966
The Kids Are Alright – August 1966
La-La-La-Lies – November 1966
Happy Jack – December 1966
Pictures of Lily – April 1967
The Last Time – July 1967
I Can See for Miles – October 1967
Dogs – June 1968
Magic Bus – July 1968
Pinball Wizard – March 1969
I'm Free – July 1969
The Acid Queen 1969
Christmas 1969
Go to the Mirror! 1969
The Seeker – April 1970
See Me, Feel Me – September 1970
Won't Get Fooled Again – June 1971

Behind Blue Eyes – October 1971
Let's See Action – November 1971
Relay – December 1972
5.15 – September 1973
Squeeze Box – November 1975
Who Are You – July 1978
Long Live Rock – April 1979
I'm One 1979
Don't Let Go the Coat – May 1981

ROGER DALTREY SOLO ALBUMS

DALTREY
April 1973

Side One:
One Man Band
The Way of the World
You Are Yourself
Thinking
You and Me

Side Two:
Hard Life
Giving It All Away
The Story So Far
When the Music Stops
Reasons
One Man Band (reprise)

RIDE A ROCK HORSE
June 1975

Side One:
Come and Get Your Love
Hearts Right

Oceans Away
Proud
World Over

Side Two:
Near to Surrender
Feeling
Walking the Dog
Milk Train
I Was Born to Sing Your Song

ONE OF THE BOYS
May 1977

Side One:
Parade
Single Man's Dilemma
Avenging Annie
The Prisoner
Leon

Side Two:
One of the Boys
Giddy
Say It Ain't So, Joe
Satin and Lace
Doing It All Again

PARTING SHOULD BE PAINLESS
February 1984

Side One:
Walking in My Sleep
Parting Would Be Painless
Is There Anybody Out There
Would a Stranger Do
Going Strong

Side Two:
Looking for You
Somebody Told Me
One Day
How Does the Cold Wind Cry
Don't Wait on the Stairs

UNDER A RAGING MOON
October 1985

Don't Talk to Strangers
Breaking Down Paradise
The Pride You Hide
Move Better in the Night
Let Me Down Easy
Fallen Angel
It Don't Satisfy Me
Rebel
Under a Raging Moon

CAN'T WAIT TO SEE THE MOVIE
June 1987

Hearts of Fire
When the Thunder Comes
Are You Ready for Love
Balance on Wires
Miracle of Love
The Price of Love
The Heart Has Its Reasons
Alone in the Night
Lover's Storm
Take Me Home

ROCKS IN THE HEAD
July 1992

Who's Gonna Walk on Water
Before My Time Is Up
Times Changed (co-writer Roger Daltrey)
You Can't Call It Love (co-writer Roger Daltrey)
Mirror Mirror
Perfect World
Love Is (co-writer Roger Daltrey)
Blues Man's Road (co-writer Roger Daltrey)
Everything a Heart Could Ever Want
Days of Light (co-writer Roger Daltrey)
Unforgettable Opera (co-writer Roger Daltrey)

MARTYRS AND MADMEN – THE BEST OF ROGER DALTREY
July 1997

One Man Band
It's a Hard Life
Giving It All Away
Thinking
World Over
Oceans Away
One of the Boys
Avenging Annie
Say It Ain't So, Joe
Parade
Free Me
Without Your Love
Waiting for a Friend
Walking in My Sleep
Parting Should Be Painless

After the Fire
Let Me Down Easy
Pride You Hide
Under a Raging Moon (single version)
Lover's Storm

ANTHOLOGY
August 2002

Giving It All Away
Thinking
It's a Hard Life
One Man Band
Get Your Love
Walking the Dog
Written on the Wind
Say It Ain't So Joe
One of the Boys
Avenging Annie
Free Me
Without Your Love
Waiting for a Friend
Walking in My Sleep
Parting Should Be Painless
After the Fire
Under a Raging Moon
Pride You Hide
Let Me Down Easy
Hearts of Fire

FILM MUSIC BY ROGER DALTREY

LISZTOMANIA
October 1975

Roger Daltrey sings:
Love's Dream (Liszt/lyrics Daltrey)
Orpheus Song (music and lyrics Daltrey)
Funérailles (Liszt/lyrics Daltrey)
Peace at Last (music and lyrics Daltrey)

McVICAR (film soundtrack)
June 1980

Side One:
Bitter and Twisted
Just a Dream Away
Escape Part One
White City Lights
Free Me

Side Two:
My Time Is Gonna Come
Waiting for a Friend
Escape Part Two
Without Your Love
McVicar

SOLO SINGLES BY ROGER DALTREY

Giving It All Away – April 1973
I'm Free – June 1973
Thinking – September 1973
It's a Hard Life – November 1973
Listening to You – See Me, Feel Me – March 1975

Come and Get Your Love – May 1975
Walking the Dog – July 1975
Orpheus Song – October 1975
Oceans Away – November 1975
Written on the Wind – April 1977
One of the Boys – May 1977
Say It Ain't So, Joe – August 1977
Avenging Annie – September 1977
Leon – 1978
Free Me – June 1980
Without Your Love – September 1980
Waiting for a Friend – 1980
Martyrs and Madmen – April 1982
Walking in My Sleep – February 1984
Parting Should Be Painless – June 1984
After the Fire – September 1985
Let Me Down Easy – December 1985
Under a Raging Moon – February 1986
Quicksilver Lightning – April 1986
The Pride You Hide – May 1986
Hearts of Fire – June 1987
Don't Let the Sun Go Down on Me – July 1987

Index

PICTURE CREDITS

p.1 Rex Features; p.2 Rex Features (bottom); p.3 Pictorial Press (bottom); p.4 Mirrorpix (bottom); p.5 Pictorial Press (top), Michael Ochs Archives/Redferns (bottom); p.6 Rex Features (top), Pictorial Press (bottom); p.7 Getty Images (top and bottom); p.8 Jan Olofsson/Redferns (top), Pictorial Press (bottom); p. 9 Rex Features (top and bottom); p. 10 Rex Features (top), Pictorial Press (bottom); p. 11 Neal Preston/CORBIS (bottom); p. 12 Pictorial Press (top left), Rex Features (top right), Rex Features (bottom); p. 13 Rex Features (top), Mirrorpix (bottom); p. 14 Rex Features (top), The History Channel (bottom); p. 15 Hulton-Deutsch Collection/CORBIS (top), Getty Images (bottom); p.16 Richard Young/Rex